What Would a Muslim Say?

What Would a Muslim Say?

Conversations, Questions, and Answers about Islam

by

Ahmed Lotfy Rashed

Common Word Publishing
"With Dialogue Comes Understanding"

Copyright

Editing: Allister Thompson

Cover Design: Stewart Williams

ISBN–13: 978-1-943740-16-1

Dedication

In the Name of God,
the Most-Gracious,
the Ever-Merciful

Acknowledgments

There are many people to thank for this book:

First, I thank my mother for teaching me always to be patient, even if it is uncomfortable. And I thank my father for teaching me to always be truthful, even if it is unpopular.

Second, I thank my wife for her patience, support, and encouragement as I navigated each conversation.

Last but certainly not least, I want to thank the shining models whom I consulted or referenced for the more nuanced or detailed answers that I had to provide. Thank you, Zaid Shakir, Hamza Yusuf, Nouman Ali Khan, Suhaib Webb, Sherman Jackson, and Jamal Badawi. May God bless you all and preserve your teachings for all students of Islam.

Contents

Copyright..iv

Dedication.. v

Acknowledgments..vi

Contents vii

Foreword.. ix

Preface x

Introduction... 3

    The Conversations Begin....................................... 4

Conversation With Dustin.. 7

    The Qur'an and How it Informs a Muslim's Faith...... 7

Conversation With Robby 19

    Faith, Sex, and Marriage in Islam........................... 19

Conversation With Barbara 25

    How a Muslim Should Respond to Criticism 25

Conversation With Jessica 31

    Jihad and Freedom in the Modern World................. 31

Conversation With Bernie 45

    Islamic Worship, Prayer, Charity, and Pilgrimage..... 45

Conversation With Satish 53

    Salvation and Tolerance in Islam............................. 53

Conversation With Jessica - Part 2 61

    Muslim Culture and Modernity................................ 61

Conversation With Jessica – Part 3............................. 73

    Understanding Islamic Law..................................... 73

Conversation With Marlene... 89

    Etiquettes of Visiting a Mosque 89

Conversation With Winston... 93

    God's Grace and Free Will 93

Conversation With Lilian 107

    Are Islamic Rulings Static or Dynamic? 107

Conversation With Riley 115

    How Can Islam be Called a Religion of Peace? 115

Conversation With Eoin 125

    Can Muslims and Christians Ever Live in Harmony? 125

A Message From the Author... 133

The Qur'an Discussions 135

About the Author xii

Online References xiii

Print References xiv

Foreword

The 877-WHY-ISLAM project was launched in 1999 by volunteers associated with Islamic Circle of North America (I.C.N.A.). It derives inspiration from the following Qur'anic verse: "Call them to the path of your Lord with wisdom and words of good advice; and reason with them in the best way. Your Lord surely knows who has strayed from His path, and He surely knows who are rightly guided." Qur'an (16:125)

The project's foremost aim is to provide accurate information about Islam, the fastest-growing religion in the world, which is practiced by over 1.6 billion people across the globe. In doing so, it hopes to dispel popular stereotypes and persistent misconceptions about Islam and Muslims.

WhyIslam uses many different channels to spread the message, including both digital (like social media) and more traditional (like billboard ads on major highways). What all these have in common is the contributions of many dedicated volunteers. Without these volunteers, there really would be no WhyIslam. It gives me great pleasure to introduce Ahmed Rashed, who has been one of our main volunteers in the Email One to One Correspondence channel. This channel is described to people requesting it as:

We are assigning one of our volunteers to email you. That person will be your primary, personal contact for any and all information about Islam and will always be just an email away. Whether you have general questions about Islam, need clarifications on Islamic issues, or are just curious to learn more, your correspondent will be the one to help you.

Ahmed, by the grace of Allah, has done some amazing work over the years, and I hope and pray that this book provides benefit to both Muslims involved in the call to Islam and to non-Muslims wanting to understand more about Islam.

Hamayon F. Khan
Why Islam Email Correspondence Manager
Piscataway, NJ

Preface

This book documents my experiences as a volunteer with WhyIslam.org. Since 2009, I have helped facilitate dialogue with many different people, answering questions about Islam and addressing misconceptions about my faith. While many of the conversations were simple question-answer sessions, quite a few were deep and engaging dialogues. I felt that it would be a great loss if these interactions remained out of the public sphere, so I wrote this book to share those conversations with people who might otherwise not have the ability or opportunity to talk with a Muslim about the beliefs of our faith.

Over the course of these dialogues, I compiled an extensive list of resources, documents, and other information that has benefited my conversation partners. I have written this book in part to share reliable, authentic, quality resources for those seeking information and those who would like to know which sources are reliable and reputable in a simple way.

My hope is that this book can be a small step toward better understanding and harmony.

TOP 15 TOUGH QUESTIONS ON ISLAM

AHMED LOTFY RASHED

Get your FREE copy when you sign up to the author's email list!

GET IT HERE:
www.WhatWouldAMuslimSay.net

MY TEACHER WAS AHMED RASHED. WE SPENT A LOT OF TIME GOING THROUGH THE QUR'AN. AFTER THAT I STARTED TO UNDERSTAND MUSLIMS MUCH BETTER. —FORMER ISLAM-101 STUDENT

What Would
a Muslim Say?

INTRODUCTION

The Conversations Begin

This book contains conversations with people who reached out to WhyIslam.org for dialogue and received me as their correspondent. WhyIslam conversations typically begin when a person visits the WhyIslam website and submits a "One to One Email Correspondence" form. From this form, the Correspondence Manager assigns the visitor to one of the WhyIslam volunteers. If the visitor is assigned to me, the questions or comments are delivered to my email, and then I initiate the first email to reach out and respond to the visitor's questions. The conversation then flows from there, just like a print letter correspondence. New questions, topics, and ideas are shared and discussed as they come up.

The book contains conversations from 2009 to 2011. Often, conversations overlap between people, but for ease of reading, I have collected conversations with one person and put them in chronological order, from first to last.

With some conversation partners, there is a break in conversation that is restarted later. These conversations are marked with "Part 2" or "Part 3" to indicate it is a continuation of a prior established conversation. Other times, at the end of the conversation, there is no further follow-up.

The conversations in this book are real. They are faithful transcripts of email correspondence that I have had with WhyIslam.org visitors over the years. To protect the privacy of our visitors, the names and identifying details have been changed. For those who restarted the conversation at a later time, their name is preserved to show continuity in conversation partners. When initiating a new conversation, I always send a standard opening email. That email is reproduced here for reference.

Standard Email Introduction

Email #01 – From: Ahmed Rashed

In the Name of God, the Most-Gracious, the Ever-Merciful:

Thank you for taking the time to contact us and learn about Islam straight from the source. We practice and promote a balanced view of Islam — the "middle way" that the Qur'an calls Muslims to follow: a path of moderation that is free of *extremism*.

Before we begin, let me introduce myself. My name is Ahmed Rashed. I am a volunteer for WhyIslam.org. I was born in Egypt but raised in America. I am married with two little children. I work as a test software engineer, but my life's passion is teaching others about Islam.

Now I'm going to give you a brief description of what Islam is all about: Islam is not a new religion. Rather, it is the same truth that God revealed through all His prophets to every people. For over a fifth of the world's population, Islam is both a religion and a complete way of life. Muslims are taught to be truthful, to be just, to help the needy, to honor their parents, and to maintain good relations with neighbors and relatives.

The Qur'an tells Muslims to say: **"We believe in God and what was revealed to us, and what was revealed to Abraham and Ishmael and Isaac and Jacob and the Tribes, and what was given to Moses and Jesus and to the Prophets from their Lord. We do not separate between them, and to Him we submit."** (3:84)

This is how Islam sees itself in relation to all other religions. The Message revealed to Muhammad is considered God's religion for humanity in its final form. Muslims view Muhammad as the final successor to Jesus, Moses, Abraham, and all the previous prophets. Muslims view the Qur'an as the final Testament from God to humanity. Just as God sent revelation to Moses and Jesus (peace be upon them), Muslims believe God sent revelation to Muhammad (peace be upon him) to confirm, correct, and complete all previous Scriptures.

The Qur'an says that God sent prophets to every community in history. These prophets were men of high moral character chosen by God to teach their people about their duty to God and to their fellow man. The Qur'an teaches that this duty was always "submission and devotion to God" and to treat all God's creation with equality and compassion.

"*Islam*" is simply the Arabic word for this duty of "submission and devotion" to God.

"*Muslim*" is the Arabic word for "one who submits" to God and obeys Him.

The Qur'an says that whenever a people broke away from God's teachings, God would send another prophet to bring them back to His Path. This is how Muslims understand the many prophets sent to the Children of Israel and the many religions in the world today.

Prophet Muhammad, like all the prophets before him, called people to believe in and worship One God, to believe in His Angels, to believe in His Prophets, to believe in His Revelations, to believe in the Day of Judgment, and to believe in Divine Decree and Destiny.

Prophet Muhammad, like all the prophets before him, called people to bear witness that there is no god but God and that he was God's Messenger, to pray regularly, to give charity regularly, and to fast as a form of self-purification. Prophet Muhammad, like Prophet Abraham before him, called people to make the pilgrimage to the Holy Sanctuary in Mecca, where the first house of worship dedicated to God Almighty was built.

This is just a general overview, so please reply with any questions you may have. I look forward to your response, and I hope to continue the discussion.

May peace be with you,
Ahmed Rashed

CONVERSATION WITH DUSTIN

The Qur'an and How it Informs a Muslim's Faith

Email #02 – From: Dustin
Sent: Sunday, September 13, 2009 6:11 a.m.
To: Ahmed Rashed

Hey! Thanks for getting in touch with me. I have actually signed up for a lot of Islamic sites and never heard anything from anyone. So, really, thank you so much. Yes, I would love to start the One-to-One Email Correspondence as soon as possible. Just show me where to start and what to do.

Thanks again,

Dustin

Email #03 – From: Ahmed Rashed
Sent: Sunday, September 13, 2009 2:54 p.m.
To: Dustin

Hey Dustin,

As I mentioned before, we give a brief overview of the beliefs and practice of Islam. Then we go into more details based on the questions you ask in the first email. We keep going deeper and more detailed with each email exchange until you feel satisfied that you've learned enough about Islam.

Beliefs: We are known as one of the three great Abrahamic faiths. Like Judaism and Christianity, our religion was founded by a descendant of Abraham. We believe in Moses and Jesus (peace be upon them) and the original Torah and Gospel as revealed to the Prophets. We believe in the Ten Commandments.

We believe in God, His angels, His scriptures and prophets, the Day of Judgment and heaven and hell, and in God's Wise Decree and Measure, and Man's free will. These are the basic articles of Islamic faith. Anybody who denies any one of these is no longer considered a Muslim.

Some people think we have a different God because we use the Arabic language name for God, "Allah." Whether we are Christians, Jews, or Muslims, we all pray to the same God. We believe God sent a messenger to every nation with the same message: Believe in one God and be good to each other.

What Would a Muslim Say?

We are taught that Islam is just the final brick in the house that God has built through his other prophets.

One becomes a Muslim by declaring there is only one God (thus, no one should play God) and Muhammad is his messenger.

Duties: A Muslim is required to pray five times a day, pay charity every year to help the needy, fast during the month of Ramadan, and make the pilgrimage to Mecca if we are able.

This is a very brief overview. After you read this, reply with any questions you have, and we can move forward from there.

May peace be with you,
Ahmed

Email #04 – From: Dustin
Sent: Sunday, September 13, 2009 11:46 p.m.
To: Ahmed Rashed

Okay, I don't know really what to start on first. But I would like to learn about the Qur'an, and if it can be proven to truly be from God. The reason I'm starting there is because of all the research on the "bible" I have done over the years. It's left me disappointed. I don't believe the bible to be the word of God anymore. But it's whatever you would like to teach me first.

Thanks again,
Dustin

Email #05 – From: Ahmed Rashed
Sent: Monday, September 14, 2009 6:17 a.m.
To: Dustin

No problem, Dustin. Actually, the Qur'an is a very good place to start because it is the main source of guidance and wisdom and law in Islam. It is the bedrock of Islam. Please forgive the length of this email; my wish is to give you a thorough and deep look at the Final Testament from God to humanity, the Qur'an.

What is the Qur'an?

The Qur'an is the primary source of every Muslim's faith and practice. Its basic theme is the relationship between God and His creatures. At the same time, it provides guidelines and detailed teachings for a just society, proper human conduct, and an equitable economic system.

The compilation and preservation of the Qur'an

Muslims believe the Qur'an is the literal word of God. They believe it was revealed to His Prophet Muhammad through the Angel Gabriel. It was memorized by Muhammad, who then dictated it to his Companions. They, in turn, memorized it, wrote it down, and reviewed it with the Prophet Muhammad during his lifetime. Moreover, the Prophet Muhammad reviewed the Qur'an with the Angel Gabriel once each year. In the last year of his life, the Prophet reviewed the Qur'an with the Angel Gabriel twice.

From the time the Qur'an was revealed until this day, there has always been a huge number of Muslims who have memorized all of the Qur'an, letter by letter. By the time the Prophet died, there were over **100 Companions** who had the entire Qur'an memorized, some of them as young as fourteen. Not one letter of the Qur'an has been changed over the centuries. It is the ONLY scripture in the world that can truthfully claim to be the same today as it was originally. It is the ONLY scripture in the world that is regularly memorized by its followers (even by non-Arabic speakers).

The Qur'an's preservation

Below is an excerpt that shows how even non-Muslim scholars (some of whom are virulently anti-Islam) admit that the Qur'an we have today is the Qur'an that Muhammad taught his Companions. **Note:** the word **Ahadith** means **"oral traditions"** in Arabic and the word **mushaf** means **"codex"** in Arabic.

...many orientalists themselves have admitted like Gibb that "It seems reasonably well established that no material changes were introduced and that the original form of Mohammed's discourses were preserved with scrupulous precision" [36]. John Burton, at the end of his substantial work on the Qur'an's compilation, says with reference to

criticisms made of different readings narrated in **Ahadith** that "No major differences of doctrines can be constructed on the basis of the parallel readings based on the Uthmanic consonantal outline, yet ascribed to **mushafs** other than his. All the rival readings unquestionably represent one and the same text. They are substantially agreed in what they transmit..." [37]. He further states that the Qur'an as we have it today is "the text which has come down to us in the form in which it was organized and approved by the Prophet.... What we have today in our hands is the **mushaf** of Muhammad." [38]. Kenneth Cragg describes the transmission of the Qur'an from the time of revelation to today as occurring in "an unbroken living sequence of devotion" [39]. Schwally concurs that "As far as the various pieces of revelation are concerned, we may be confident that their text has been generally transmitted exactly as it was found in the Prophet's legacy" [40].

[36] H.A.R. Gibb, **Mohammedanism**, London: Oxford University Press, 1969, p. 50.

[37] John Burton, **The Collection of the Qur'an**, Cambridge: Cambridge University Press, 1977, p. 171.

[38] John Burton, **The Collection of the Qur'an**, Cambridge: Cambridge University Press, 1977, p. 239-40.

[39] Kenneth Cragg, **The Mind of the Qur'an**, London: George Allen & Unwin, 1973, p. 26.

[40] Schwally, **Geschichte des Qorans**, Leipzig: Dieterich'sche Verlagsbuchhandlung, 1909-38, Vol.2, p. 120.

The full article is here (warning, very long):

http://www.ilaam.net/Articles/AuthenticQur'an.html

Why a person would believe in the Qur'an

There are several reasons; I'll mention only three.

FIRST: As mentioned above, the Qur'an has not changed since the time of Muhammad, not even the language and pronunciation. Even non-Muslims admit this point, and those same non-Muslims admit that the Bible has certainly changed (in language, substance, and meaning) since the time of Jesus.

SECOND: The Qur'an teaches that the previous scriptures, especially the Torah of Moses and the Evangel of Jesus, foretold the coming of Muhammad. Even though the Bible we have now is not 100% what was revealed to these two Prophets, there are still remnants of these predictions of Muhammad. Check the following link (chapter 1 section 3): http://www.islam-guide.com/frm-ch1-3.htm.

THIRD: The Qur'an itself is a miracle whose only explanation is Divine Authorship. Every prophet came with a miracle to prove his credentials. Muhammad's primary miracle was the Qur'an. Why? Because unlike the raising of the dead or the parting of the sea, this miracle lives on long after the prophet is gone.

The Qur'an challenges its reader: how could an **illiterate** man living in an **ignorant** society come up with a discourse of such wisdom and eloquence? How could an **illiterate** man living in an **isolated** society come up with a discourse that refers to past nations, future events, and the natural world around us **without making a single error whatsoever?** The following link is a review of the miraculous nature of the Qur'an by Dr. Gary Miller, an atheist turned Christian turned minister turned Muslim: http://www.islam101.com/science/GaryMiller.html.

Conclusion: I've tried my best to give you a description of the Qur'an and its credentials. The links provided are to deepen your knowledge, and I strongly recommend you read them. Each link is a gem worth uncovering.

Anything good that came from this email is from God Almighty, and anything bad is only from my own shortcomings. Please feel free to ask any more questions, Dustin. I look forward to continuing our discussion. May God accept our efforts.

May peace be with you,
Ahmed

Email #06 – From: Dustin
Sent: Thursday, September 17, 2009 11:21 a.m.
To: Ahmed Rashed

Assalam-o-Alaikum

Now that was a good study! I am convinced that I won't be disappointed this time. Thank you for all that information. I am, though, truly convinced that the Qur'an is the word of Allah. My wife and I like to see for ourselves if things will stand our little investigation, and the Qur'an did exactly that.

I do have a few questions, though. 1. I have a friend on MySpace who lives in CA, USA. He was good enough to send me some books on Islam. I was wondering, since I am new to Islam, what could I do in return for him. I did offer to repay his money for sending me the books. But I would like to send him a gift. Could you recommend something?

2. I know to read the Qur'an through as much as possible. But as for studying, there is a book called *What Islam Is All About* that he sent me. Should I start studying that book first?

3. Does Allah draw you to him? What I mean by that is for a long time now, people — not really knowing — have given me movies with Islamic things in them. I would get books that mention something about Islam. A plate that I later discovered had Islamic writings on it. I bought the movie *Ali* and discovered that one of my favorite boxers was Muslim. And at last, by typing in the wrong address, I found a talk by "Yusuf" on YouTube and have been hooked ever since. I had never heard of Islam before all of this. Does Allah draw people like that?

4. I saw somewhere that Saudi Arabia is racist and that this is why Malcolm X was disillusioned when he went on the pilgrimage (Hajj). Could you comment?

Thanks again,

Dustin

Email #07 – From: Ahmed Rashed
Sent: Friday, September 18, 2009 6:57 a.m.
To: Dustin

Wa alaikumu salaam. I am glad to read such a positive response from you. Let's get right to your questions:

1. The best gift is a prayer for the one you care about. Personally, if it were me, I would pass on the information you learned about Islam to those around you. Knowing that the information I gave to you was being passed on to others would be the greatest gift I could ever receive.

2. That book is an excellent introduction and reference book on Islam. It has many excerpts from the Qur'an and the sayings of the Prophet. Also, it gives you references to the Qur'an for each topic it covers. That way, you can read the book and have an English Qur'an next to you to see the source of whatever point is being discussed.

3. Yes, definitely. There is an African-American brother here who is now the Imam of a masjid. He said he started getting interested in Islam when he saw the Qur'an in a dream. Another saw Jesus in a dream, telling him to be Muslim. Here is a link to a few conversion stories:
http://islamicweb.com/begin/newMuslims/.

4. I am not sure where you got this idea. First of all, Islam has always been color-blind and egalitarian. As for Malcolm X, here is what he told Alex Haley in his autobiography:

"Never have I witnessed such sincere hospitality and such overwhelming spirit of true brotherhood as is practiced by people of all colors and races here in this Ancient Holy Land, the home of Abraham and all the other Prophets of Holy scriptures. For the past week I have been truly speechless and spellbound by the graciousness I see displayed all around me by people of all colors. I have been blessed to visit the Holy City of Mecca ... There were tens of thousands of pilgrims, from all over the world. They were of all colors, from blue eyed blonds to black skinned Africans. But we were all practicing in the same ritual, displaying a spirit of unity and brotherhood that my experiences in America had led

me to believe never could exist between the white and the non-white.

America needs to understand Islam, because this is the one religion that erases from its society the race problem. Throughout my travels in the Muslim world, I have met, talked to, even eaten with people who in America would have been considered white, but the white attitude had been removed from their minds by the religion of Islam. I have never before seen such sincere and true brotherhood, practiced by all colors together, irrespective of their color.

You may be shocked by these words coming from me. But on this pilgrimage, what I have seen and experienced has forced me to rearrange much of the thought patterns previously held, and to toss aside some of my previous conclusions. Despite my firm convictions, I have always been a man who tries to face facts, and to accept the reality of life as new experience and new knowledge unfolds. I have always kept an open mind, a flexibility that must go hand in hand with every form of the intelligent search for truth.

I could see from this, that perhaps if white Americans could accept the Oneness of God, then perhaps, too, they could accept in reality the oneness of man and cease to measure, and hinder, and harm others in terms of their differences in color."

May peace be with you,
Ahmed

Email #08 – From: Dustin
Sent: Tuesday, September 22, 2009 1:51 p.m.
To: Ahmed Rashed

Assalam-o-Alaikum

Thank you for your reply and helping with the questions I had, especially the one about Malcolm. I have always loved the teachings of Malcolm X. It was just a video I saw, trying to twist Malcolm's words. Could give me a chapter outline of the Qur'an?

I want to know where to go and what to read in certain situations. For example, the first chapter is about how we should praise him, that kind of thing. I have looked online, but I didn't find anything.

QUESTIONS:

1. Did the prophet Jesus (Pbuh) die on the cross like the churches teach?

2. What exactly do I say and do while I am praying to Allah? I mean, are there ways that I should place my hands? Are there words that need to be said?

3. Is there another book that I should have as a companion along with the Qur'an?

Well, there are my questions for today!

No really, thank you for taking time out to do these studies with me. You have been a lot of help. I look forward to your answers.

Thanks again,

Dustin

Email #09 – From: Ahmed Rashed
Sent: Tuesday, September 22, 2009 2:51 p.m.
To: Dustin

Assalaamu alaikum,

You are quite welcome, Dustin; I am at your service. A chapter outline of the Qur'an is not really feasible. That is because each chapter touches on many subjects, and many subjects are given a slightly different presentation in each chapter that they appear. This is because the Qur'an is a conversation between the Lord and His creation; so this conversation spans many topics in each chapter, and in each chapter, the Lord reminds and reiterates certain themes or stories that are useful to His creatures. It is meant to be read from front to back many times during a person's life. It is also meant that a man can open the book anywhere in the middle and start a spiritual conversation with his Creator.

However, there is a decent topic index here:
http://www.islamicity.com/mosque/TOPICI.HTM.

You can also find a decent hyperlinked translation of the Qur'an here:
http://www.islamicity.com/mosque/Surai.htm.

Now for your questions:

1. The Qur'an describes it this way: **For they rejected Faith; for they uttered against Mary a grave false charge; For they said, "We killed the Christ, Jesus the son of Mary, the Messenger of Allah." But they killed him not, nor crucified him, but so it was made to appear to them. And those who differ therein are full of doubts, with no knowledge, but only conjecture to follow, for of a surety they killed him not.**

Nay, Allah raised him up unto Himself; and Allah is Exalted in Power, Wise; And there is none of the People of the Book but must believe in him before his death; and on the Day of Judgment he will be a witness against them. (4:156-159)

2. It is preferable to have a Muslim teach you in person.

3. "Should" have? No. The Qur'an is sufficient for everyday needs. Other books and learning are really only needed for those who want to derive Islamic law or who want commentary on obscure Arabic references. Sometimes it is good to have an annotated Qur'an that explains the occasions of each chapter's revelations. This will give you the specific context of the verses, but the general meanings are still accessible without commentary. Let me know if you have any other questions.

May peace be with you,
Ahmed

With Dialogue Comes Understanding

CONVERSATION WITH ROBBY

Faith, Sex, and Marriage in Islam

Email #02 – From: Robby
Sent: Thursday, October 18, 2009 11:01 a.m.
To: Ahmed Rashed

Thanks for the intro. Could you go in-depth about the beliefs and rituals of Islam?

Thank you,
Robby

Email #03 – From: Ahmed Rashed
Sent: Monday, October 19, 2009 2:46 p.m.
To: Robby

We will start our discussion with the basic articles of faith. They are:

1. Belief in God
2. Belief in His Angels
3. Belief in His Revelations
4. Belief in His Prophets
5. Belief in the Day of Judgment
6. Belief in Divine Predestination

We will discuss them one at a time, answering all questions about the first before we move on to the next.

The Basic Islamic Beliefs

1) Belief in God:

Muslims believe in one, unique, incomparable God, who has neither son nor partner, and that none has the right to be worshipped but Him alone. He is the true God, and every other deity is false. He has the most magnificent names and sublime, perfect attributes. No one shares His divinity or His attributes. In the Qur'an, God describes Himself: **Say, "He is God, the One. God, the Absolute. He begets not, nor was He begotten, and there is none like Him. (112:1-4)**

No one has the right to be invoked, supplicated, prayed to, or shown any act of worship but God alone.

God alone is the Almighty, the Creator, the Sovereign, and the Sustainer of everything in the whole universe. He manages all affairs. He stands in need of none of His creatures, and all His creatures depend on Him for all that they need. He is the All-Hearing, the All-Seeing, and the All-Knowing. In a perfect manner, His knowledge encompasses all things, the open and the secret, and the public and the private. He knows what has happened, what will happen, and how it will happen. No affair occurs in the whole world except by His will. Whatever He wills is, and whatever He does not will is not and will never be. His will is above the will of all the creatures. He has power over all things, and He is able to do everything. He is the Most Gracious, the Most Merciful, and the Most Beneficent. In one of the sayings of the Prophet Muhammad, we are told that *God is more merciful to His creatures than a mother to her child.* God is far removed from injustice and tyranny. He is All-Wise in all of His actions and decrees. If someone wants something from God, he or she can ask God directly without asking anyone else to intercede with God for him or her.

Islam teaches that God is not Jesus, and Jesus is not God. The Qur'an says: **Indeed, they have disbelieved who have said, "God is the Messiah, son of Mary." The Messiah said, "Children of Israel, worship God, my Lord and your Lord. Whoever associates partners in worship with God, then God has forbidden Paradise for him, and his home is the Fire. For the wrongdoers, there will be no helpers. (5:72)**

Indeed, they disbelieve who say, "God is the third of three," when there is no god but one God. If they desist not from what they say, truly, a painful punishment will befall the disbelievers among them. Would they not rather repent to God and ask His forgiveness? For God is Oft-Forgiving, Most Merciful. The Messiah, son of Mary, was no more than a messenger. (5:73-75)

Islam rejects that God rested on the seventh day of the creation, that He wrestled with one of His angels, that He is an envious plotter against mankind, or that He is incarnate in any human being. Islam also rejects the attribution of any human form to God. All of these are considered blasphemous. God is the

Exalted. He is far removed from every imperfection. He never becomes weary. He does not become drowsy, nor does he sleep.

The Arabic word Allah means God (the one and only true God who created the whole universe). This word "Allah" is a name for God, which is used by Arabic speakers, both Arab Muslims and Arab Christians. This word cannot be used to designate anything other than the one true God. The Arabic word Allah occurs in the Qur'an about 2700 times. In Aramaic, a language related closely to Arabic and the language that Jesus habitually spoke, God is also referred to as Allah.

Read and ponder this selection, then reply with any and all questions that come to mind. I apologize for the length, but this is the single most important belief in Islam.

May peace be with you,
Ahmed

Email #04 – From: Robby
Sent: Tuesday, October 20, 2009 11:21 a.m.
To: Ahmed Rashed

Can you tell me about sex and marriage please?
Thank you.

Email #05 – From: Ahmed Rashed
Sent: Wednesday, October 21, 2009 10:16 a.m.
To: Robby

That's a big jump from beliefs and worship!

I assume you understood belief in God. Belief in the angels, the prophets, the revealed scriptures, the Day of Judgment, and Divine Decree are the other articles of faith. I will continue sending these to you, God-willing, so we can be assured you have all accurate information.

After that, we should talk about the pillars of worship: Testifying that there is no god but God and that Muhammad is His messenger, praying five times a day, fasting during month of Ramadan, making the pilgrimage to Mecca at least once in your life, and giving charity if you possess more than eighty-five grams of gold (or their equivalent in local currency and liquid assets) for a full lunar year.

After that, we can start talking about lifestyle! Usually, we talk about five topics in this section: rules for speech and behavior, rules for earning and spending, rules for love and marriage, rules for eating and drinking, and finally rules for games and leisure.

Since you have asked directly, I will explain the Islamic etiquettes of love, sex, and marriage. God says in the Qur'an **"And do no approach adultery; it is immoral and an evil way."** (17:32) From this, we understand that not only is sex outside of marriage a sin, but even coming near to this act is itself a sin. For this reason, the Prophet instructed his community to be very careful around the opposite sex. Flirting, joking, patting, hugging, kissing, and close friendship is not considered appropriate between a man and a woman unless the two in question are related or married to each other.

A man and woman are allowed to interact with each other in a business, educational, political, or medical situation, but all these interactions **must** be with professional detachment and propriety. That means that personal space is not transgressed and personal conversation is not held.

Most of what goes on in the Western world regarding the mixing and socializing between men and women is considered sinful or at best un-Islamic. Islam defines fidelity and chastity as not just **sexual** exclusivity, but also **physical** exclusivity and **emotional** exclusivity. Most people in the West have evolved the opinion that as long as a man only has sex with his wife, he may get physical and emotional with other women.

Islam takes the comprehensive and pragmatic view that emotions and physicality often lead to intimacy and sexuality; therefore, Islam commands its followers to follow the purer route and keep themselves fully chaste for their spouses only.

May peace be with you,
Ahmed

Email #06 – From: Robby
Sent: Thursday, October 22, 2009 11:01 a.m.
To: Ahmed Rashed

Thanks. How old do you have to be to get married?
Thank you,
Robby

Email #07 – From: Ahmed Rashed
Sent: Friday, October 23, 2009 11:49 a.m.
To: Robby

There is no age limit for marriage in Islam. Muslims are encouraged to marry young to avoid the temptation of adultery and sexual frustration. The only hard and fast minimum requirements for a valid marriage are that both bride and groom must have physically matured. This means the girl must have demonstrated menstruation and the boy must have demonstrated ejaculation. This is the absolute minimum.

However, in addition, the groom **must** be able to feed, clothe, shelter, and maintain his wife, so this usually means that man doesn't marry until after graduating high school or college. Also, the bride usually requires the consent of her guardians, so this usually means that she doesn't marry until after high school, although I know of people in the Middle East (mainly farmers and country folk) who marry their girls as young as thirteen or fourteen. If the woman has married before, or she is a convert, consent of the family is strongly recommended but not required.

Let me know if there are any other questions you have.
May peace be with you,
Ahmed

CONVERSATION WITH BARBARA

How a Muslim Should Respond to Criticism

Email #02 – From: Barbara
Sent: Wednesday, March 23, 2010 6:19 a.m.
To: Ahmed Rashed

I've been asking you idiots since last year for a Koran and have not received anything. I did some research on your so-called peaceful religion and discovered it is all a dictatorship and nothing else. I, for one, do not want to be associated with something as archaic and outdated as Islam. I am a Baha'i, and I'm staying where I'm at. At least in the Baha'i faith, we believe that women are equal in the eyes of God. You people treat your women like trash. They have to wear rags on their heads and over their faces, which shows how pathetic you people really are. So forget sending me the Koran, you can use it when you run out of toilet paper. Another thing, you people want to go out and kill non-believers. It only proves how demented and mentally sick you jerks really are. This is the United States of America and it will NEVER be an Islamic country.

Email #03 – From: Ahmed Rashed
Sent: Wednesday, March 24, 2010 8:11 a.m.
To: Barbara

In the Name of God, the Most-Gracious, the Ever-Merciful:
It is clear that you are very angry with us, but I pray we can come to an amicable understanding, God-willing. To proceed with your comments:

I've been asking you idiots since last year for a Koran and have not received anything.

For some reason, your request did not register in our system, so please forgive us for not sending you a Qur'an in a timely manner.

I did some research on your so-called peaceful religion and discovered it is all a dictatorship and nothing else.

Dictatorship is totally against Islamic teachings. There is a lot of propaganda and misinformation on the web. It is for this reason we launched this humble correspondence service.

The Qur'an orders the Prophet to consult with his followers: **So pardon them and implore God to forgive them. Take counsel with them in the conduct of affairs; and when you are resolved, put your trust in God. Verily God loves those who trust in Him. (3:159)**

The Qur'an also praises the community that runs its affairs with consultation: **Better and lasting is that which God has for those who believe and put their trust in Him; who avoid gross sins and lewdness; who when angered are ready to forgive; who obey their Lord, attend to their prayers, and conduct their affairs by mutual consultation; who give charity out of that which We have given them; and who when oppressed seek to redress their wrongs. (42:36-39)**

In addition, here are a few example of what *non-Muslim* scholars and intellectuals have to say about Islam and the Prophet:

"No other society has such a record of success in uniting in an equality of status, of opportunity and endeavour so many and so varied races of mankind. The great Muslim communities of Africa, India and Indonesia, perhaps also the small community in Japan, show that Islam has still the power to reconcile apparently irreconcilable elements of race and tradition. If ever the opposition of the great societies of the East and west is to be replaced by cooperation, the mediation of Islam is an indispensable condition." (H.A.R. Gibb, *Whither Islam*, p. 379)

"The extinction of race consciousness as between Muslims is one of the outstanding achievements of Islam and in the contemporary world there is, as it happens, a crying need for the propagation of this Islamic virtue..." (A.J. Toynbee, *Civilization On Trial*, p. 205)

"Sense of justice is one of the most wonderful ideals of Islam, because as I read in the Qur'an I find those dynamic principles of life, not mystic but practical ethics for the daily conduct of life suited to the whole world." —Lectures on *"The Ideals of Islam;"* see *Speeches and Writings of Sarojini Naidu*, Madras, 1918, p. 167.

"The doctrine of brotherhood of Islam extends to all human beings, no matter what color, race or creed. Islam is the only religion which has been able to realize this doctrine in practice. Muslims wherever on the world they are will recognize each other as brothers." — Mr. R. L. Mellema, Dutch anthropologist, writer, and scholar.

You can read more quotes at this link: http://www.islamicity.com/Mosque/aboutislam.htm

I, for one, do not want to be associated with something as archaic and outdated as Islam.

On the contrary, Islam is the *only* religion on the face of the Earth that is still relevant as it was originally revealed. The teachings of the Qur'an about theology, economics, ethics, and science are still true and valid as they were fourteen centuries ago.

"The essential and definite element of my conversion to Islam was the Qur'an. I began to study it before my conversion with the critical spirit of a Western intellectual. There are certain verses of this book, the Qur'an, revealed more than thirteen centuries ago, which teach exactly the same notions as the most modern scientific researchers do. This definitely converted me." —Ali Selman Benoist, French doctor of medicine.

"I have read the Sacred Scriptures of every religion; nowhere have I found what I encountered in Islam: perfection. The Holy Qur'an, compared to any other scripture I have read, is like the Sun compared to that of a match. I firmly believe that anybody who reads the Word of Allah with a mind that is not completely closed to Truth will become a Muslim." —Saifuddin Dirk Walter Mosig, U.S.A.

I am a Baha'i and I'm staying where I'm at.

You are free to do so. Our purpose is not to seek converts. Our purpose is simply to provide accurate information on our faith. There is a lot of anti-Islam propaganda and misinformation in the media. We set up this website to set the record straight; nothing more, nothing less.

At least in the Baha'i faith, we believe that women are equal in the eyes of God.

Women are equal to men in the eyes of God. The Qur'an says: **The believers who do good works, whether men or women, shall enter Paradise. They shall not suffer the least injustice. (4:123-124)**

The Prophet said: *"Women are the twin halves of men."*

You people treat your women like trash.

The Prophet and his companions treated their women like queens. The Prophet commanded his followers: *"The best of you is he who is kindest to his wives."*

A'isha (wife of the Prophet) said, "The Prophet was always at the service of his household. He would mend his own clothes and cobble his own shoes." Muslims who mistreat their women do not reflect the teachings of Islam and the Prophet.

They have to wear rags on their heads and over their faces, which shows how pathetic you people really are.

To Muslim women who practice hijab, it represents an act of obedience to God. It also represents a step towards freedom, i.e., freedom from being judged by their looks rather than their intellect.

Both men and women are required to dress and conduct themselves in a manner that befits their dignity and is not the cause of temptation for others. Hair is considered part of a woman's physical attractiveness. Therefore, covering of hair for the woman is considered essential to modesty of her attire, even in the Bible. This is the reason why nuns and orthodox Jewish women also cover their hair.

In a society where women's beauty has been made a commodity, and where women often end up associating their self-worth with their looks, the hijab and its concomitant de-emphasis of physical beauty can be tremendously liberating. Muslim women wear the hijab out of obedience to God, while recognizing the immense wisdom behind His commandment.

Another thing, you people want to go out and kill non-believers. It only proves how demented and mentally sick you jerks really are.

This is just propaganda and misinformation. The word "jihad" comes from the root word **"ja-ha-da,"** which means "struggle." At the individual level, jihad primarily refers to the inner struggle of being a person of virtue and submission to God in all aspects of life. It does nofat mean "holy war."

The Qur'an says:

There is no compulsion in religion. (2:256)

Had your Lord willed, everyone on earth would have believed. Will you compel people to become believers? (10:99)

And say, "The truth is from your Lord. Whoever wills — let him believe. And whoever wills — let him disbelieve." (18:29)

Again, I apologize for the lengthy email, but I wanted to be sure each of your issues was addressed in a complete manner. Please reply back at your earliest convenience so we may continue the discussion, for it is only through dialogue that we can attain understanding.

May peace be with you,

Ahmed Rashed

CONVERSATION WITH JESSICA

Jihad and Freedom in the Modern World

Email #02 – From: Jessica
Sent: Monday, March 22, 2010 11:35 p.m.
To: Ahmed Rashed

I really resent your slogans in the university depicting that Jesus was Islamic. No, Jesus was a Jew. I also resent you trying to recruit martyrs; perhaps you need European-looking young men to carry out your Jihad. I resent that you even mention Jihad on your website. You are the enemy living among us. You are exploiting the freedoms that we value to ultimately take it away from us. I will do everything in my power to make sure that no daughter or granddaughter of mine will have to cover themselves. God made nothing imperfect.

Email #03 – From: Ahmed Rashed
Sent: Monday, March 22, 2010 1:42 a.m.
To: Jessica

In the Name of God, the Most-Gracious, the Ever-Merciful:

I pray this email finds you in the best of health and faith, God-willing. My name is Ahmed Rashed. I am a volunteer for the WhyIslam Outreach Team, and I hope to start a dialogue with you to address the concerns you mentioned in the comments above.

To proceed with your comments:

1. *I really resent your slogans in the university depicting that Jesus was Islamic. No, Jesus was a Jew.*

He was both. Muslims believe Jesus (God's peace and blessings be upon him) was a noble Prophet and one of God's Great Messengers. Muslims agree that he was a Jew, for he was from the line David from the Children of Israel.

The Qur'an quotes Jesus (God's peace and blessings be upon him) as saying: **I am a Servant of God. He has given me the Book and made me a Prophet. He made me blessed wherever I go, and he has charged me with prayer and charity so long as I live. He has made me kind to my mother and not insolent nor miserable. So peace be upon me the day I was born and the day I die and the day I am raised to life. (19:30-33)**

What Would a Muslim Say?

The word "*islam*" is simply the Arabic word for "loving submission/obedience to God." The word "*muslim*" is simply the Arabic word for he who lovingly obeys and submits to God. Do not get confused by the language. All Prophets dedicated their whole lives to following God's Word and preaching it to their people out of love and obedience to God. In whatever language they spoke, they were all "loving devotees of God." Therefore, in the language of Arabic, they were all "*muslims*."

The Qur'an says: **He has ordained for you the Faith which He enjoined on Noah and which We have revealed to you, and which we enjoined on Abraham, Moses, and Jesus: "Observe this Faith and be not divided therein." Qur'an (42:13)**

2. I resent you trying to recruit martyrs; perhaps you need European looking young men to carry out your Jihad.

We are not trying to recruit martyrs. Our purpose is simply to provide accurate information on our faith. There is a lot of anti-Islam propaganda and misinformation in the media. We set up this website to set the record straight; nothing more, nothing less.

3. I resent that you even mention Jihad on your website.

We mention Jihad on our website because it is the most misunderstood concept in our faith. Jihad on the battlefield, in the Islamic perspective, is the last resort, and is subject to stringent conditions outlined by the Prophet: no harming of non-combatants, no demolishing buildings, no cutting down crops, and no killing of prisoners. Those are the Islamic rules of engagement.

The Qur'an says: **Permission to fight is granted to those who are attacked, because they have been wronged; God indeed has the power to help them. They are those who have been driven out of their homes unjustly, only because they said, 'Our Lord is God.' If God did not repel the aggression of some people by means of others, cloisters and churches and synagogues and mosques, wherein the name of God is much invoked, would** have been destroyed. Surely, God will help him who helps His cause; verily, God is powerful and mighty. (22:39-40)

Moreover, the Qur'an says: **And how should you not fight for the cause of God, and for the helpless old men, women, and children who say, 'Deliver us, Lord, from this city of wrongdoers, grant us a protector out of Your grace and grant us a supporter out of Your grace?' (4:75)**

Thus the conditions of physical jihad are clearly defined in the Qur'an. Regardless of how legitimate a cause may be, Islam does **not** condone the killing of innocent people.

4. You are the enemy living among us. You are exploiting the freedoms that we value to ultimately take it away from us.

How can Islam take away freedom when its whole purpose is to free mankind from physical and spiritual slavery?

Islam calls people to Guidance: **So where are you going? Verily this is but a reminder to all; to those of you who wish to be upright. Qur'an (81:26-28)**

Islam calls people to Righteousness: **Verily God commands justice and excellence and giving to kith and kin, and He forbids indecency and wickedness and oppression. He admonishes you, that ye may take heed. Qur'an (16:90)**

Islam calls people to Mercy: *"What actions are best? They are to gladden the heart of a human being, to feed the hungry, to help the afflicted, to lighten the sorrow of the sorrowful, and to remove the wrongs of the injured."* —Prophet Muhammad

Islam calls people to Compassion: *"All creatures are God's family, and those dearest to God are the ones who treat His creatures kindly."* —Prophet Muhammad

Islam calls people to accept Diversity: **And among His Signs are the creation of the heavens and the earth, and the diversity of your languages and your colors: verily in that are Signs for those with knowledge. Qur'an (30:22)**

Islam calls people to Peace: *"What is better than fasting, charity, and prayers? It is making peace between one another; for enmity and malice tear up virtue by the roots."* —Prophet Muhammad

Islam calls people to Equality:

"Women are the twin halves of men."

"All mankind is from Adam and Eve... a white man is no better than black man, and a black man is no better than a white man; except by piety and good deeds." —Prophet Muhammad

These are the **REAL** teachings of Islam.

5. I will do everything in my power to make sure that no daughter or granddaughter of mine will have to cover themselves.

To Muslim women who practice hijab, it represents an act of obedience to God. It also represents a step towards freedom, i.e., freedom from being judged by their looks rather than their intellect.

Both men and women are required to dress and conduct themselves in a manner that befits their dignity and is not the cause of temptation for others. Hair is considered part of a woman's physical attractiveness. Therefore, covering of hair for the woman is considered essential to modesty of her attire, even in the Bible. This is the reason why nuns and orthodox Jewish women also cover their hair.

In a society where women's beauty has been made a commodity, and where women often end up associating their self-worth with their looks, the hijab and its concomitant de-emphasis of physical beauty can be tremendously liberating. Muslim women wear the hijab out of obedience to God, while recognizing the immense wisdom behind His commandment.

6. God made nothing imperfect.

You have spoken truth. The Qur'an says: **Such is the handiwork of God, the One who perfected everything; and He is well aware of what you do. Qur'an (27:88)**

Islam is not a new religion. Rather, it is the same truth that God revealed through all His prophets to every people. For over a fifth of the world's population, Islam is both a religion and a complete way of life. Muslims follow a religion of peace, mercy, and forgiveness, and the majority have nothing to do with the extremely grave events which have come to be associated with their faith.

May peace be with you,
Ahmed Rashed

**Email #04 – From: Jessica
Sent: Wednesday, March 24, 2010 9:39 p.m.
To: Ahmed Rashed**

Thank you; I appreciate the dialogue.

1. If you believe we are all united in religion, why do your clerics condemn Judaism and our European and North American Christian traditions?

2. Why does your Islamic faith continue to enlist European or North American-born young men of Islamic faith to return to countries such as Somalia that their very own parents escaped? I will point out that some of the teenage or young men missing from the United States that ended up in Somalia were recruited by the very mosques that they attended. There are many examples of this. The martyrs of 9/11 were living and schooled in the United States; there have been such examples in Europe.

3. Qur'an (22:39-40) and Qur'an (4:75) – I feel this is very self-explanatory that the Qur'an teaches violence and intolerance.

4. Does this include freedom of girl children to be educated? Does this include the freedom of women to be vindicated instead of tried and sentenced in Islamic courts as the victims of rape or violence perpetrated on them by men who are not tried? Does this include the freedom of women to make their own choices without family or tribal retribution? Should the boys who are used by your Islamic followers in Afghanistan (and this has been documented practice) be free from the abuses of men, as a local tradition because they can't take the liberties they would want with women?

Did Jesus not say: whoever harms a child or takes away his innocence it is better for him that he ties a stone upon himself and throws himself in the sea, rather than face the wrath that awaits him? I also think this applies to every culture who would harm a child whether Islamic, Christian, or otherwise. Yet, it is not a cultural practice for us as it is in some Islamic countries. I would ask why you are living the same now as you did 2000 years ago. There is no progress. Even in Europe 1500 years ago the society was more advanced than your stone-age culture. There is wisdom in progression.

5. Actually, the study of theology suggests that women of Jewish and Christian faith covered their head so as not to tempt angels to fall from Heaven. Is it not accurate to say that Islamic women cover themselves to protect themselves from the eyes of the unclean, which seems to be a factor in your society?

6. Then why would you cover it? Their hair, their eyes, their beauty — why would you cut it off?? Why would Islamic cultures practice female circumcision (which is entirely different and for very different reasons than male circumcising practiced in the Jewish faith or other cultures)?

**Email #05 – From: Ahmed Rashed
Sent: Saturday, March 27, 2010 2:18 a.m.
To: Jessica**

In the Name of God, the Most-Gracious, the Ever-Merciful:
One of God's gifts to humanity is the gift of speech. It is by dialogue that we can come to greater understanding. For this reason, I am happy that you responded. Please excuse the length of this email; I wanted to answer all your questions completely.

1. First of all, there are no clerics in Islam. Each Muslim calls on God and answers to God individually with no intermediary. I think the "clerics" you refer to are the "scholars" of Islam: people who have taken the time and effort to study the Qur'an and the teachings of the Prophet and who are looked up to by virtue of their knowledge.

Secondly, regarding "condemning," Muslims believe that the Last Prophet (Muhammad) and the Last Testament (the Qur'an) were sent to **confirm**, **correct**, and *complete* the Message of all previous prophets and scriptures. It is written in the Qur'an that God sent prophets to each nation in history. In other words, God made a covenant with every people in every time. This covenant was "*Islam*," which means surrender and obedience to God, and a person who surrenders his will to God and obeys His commandments is called a "*Muslim*."

So the **original** followers of Abraham are considered Muslims by virtue of their obedience to God and the keeping of their Covenant with Him. And the **original** followers of Moses are considered Muslims by virtue of their obedience to God and the keeping of their Covenant with Him. And the **original** followers of Jesus are considered Muslims by virtue of their obedience to God and the keeping of their Covenant with Him. By the time of Muhammad (peace be upon him), there were few, if any, who were still upon the **original and pure** teachings of *any* prophet. So God sent Muhammad as the Final Messenger with the Final Revelation to guide the Arabs in particular and all of mankind in general to the correct path to their Lord and Creator.

So what this all means is that when an Islamic scholar "condemns" Judaism or Christianity, he is condemning the *changes* each previous community made to the original covenant revealed to them. He is NOT condemning the original teachings of Abraham, Moses, David, and Jesus (peace be upon them), because the teachings of Muhammad (peace be upon him) are ONE with the teachings of all the other prophets.

2. Once again, you mistakenly assume that there is some pope-like figure for the Muslims. There is not. If one group of Muslims recruits people for some evil intention, it does not mean that Islam prescribes or even condones such an action. There are good Muslims and there are bad Muslims. The definition of good Muslim and bad Muslim is what is in the Qur'an and the Sayings of the Prophet. If a Muslim does an act that the Qur'an or the Prophet say is bad, then that act is bad, and that Muslim is acting

against the teachings of Islam. All the acts that you mentioned are against the teachings of Islam. **Every major mainstream Islamic organization** *around the world* **has been** <u>condemning</u> **these kinds of acts since 9/11.** The problem, as I said before, is that the sheer volume of media propaganda and misinformation against Islam drowns out the mainstream Muslim voice.

3. I honestly cannot fathom how you could ever come to such an obviously wrong conclusion. The verses I cited are about standing up to tyranny and helping the oppressed, the weak, and the persecuted to defend themselves against aggression. It is saying that God has entrusted those who believe in Him to fight for justice in this world. Is this not the same thing that Thomas Jefferson, Andrew Jackson, Benjamin Franklin, and the other founders of the USA say in so many letters and speeches?

The Qur'an teaches that it is the obligation and responsibility of God's followers to defend the lives, homes, and faith of anyone suffering persecution. How is that teaching violence and intolerance? It is actually the Islamic understanding of armed struggle and the justification for it that led Thomas Aquinas (a famous medieval Christian philosopher) to come up with his famous concept of "Just War."

Islam teaches that men of conscience must be ready and willing to fight against injustice and persecution. It does NOT teach violence against civilians or wanton destruction of property. Those Muslims who do so are violating the teachings of the Qur'an and the Prophet.

4. Of course girls can and should get an education. The Prophet said, *"Seeking knowledge is an obligation on every Muslim, male and female."* So what you see is that Muslims are doing something that is against the teachings of Islam.

As for cases of rape of women, during the time of the Prophet, punishment was inflicted on the rapist on the solitary evidence of the woman who was raped by him. Wa'il ibn Hujr reports of an incident when a woman was raped. Later, when some people came by, she identified and accused the man of raping her. They seized him and brought him to God's Messenger, who said to the woman, *"Go away, for Allâh has forgiven you,"* but of the man who had raped her, he said, *"Stone him to death."* (Recorded by Tirmidhi and Abu Dawud)

During the time when Umar (a companion of the Prophet) was the ruler, a woman accused his son, Abu Shahmah, of raping her. She brought the infant borne of this incident with her to the mosque and publicly spoke about what had happened. Umar asked his son, who acknowledged committing the crime and was duly punished right there and then (execution). There was no punishment given to the woman. (Recorded by Rauf)

So once again, this is a case of Muslims being ignorant or negligent of the teachings of Islam.

As for women choosing their own husbands, the Prophet said, *"A matron should not be given in marriage except after consulting her; and a virgin should not be given in marriage except after her permission."*

As for cases of rape of boys, their case is the same as those who rape girls or women. Rape is a capital crime according to the teachings of Islam.

As for your quote of Jesus (pbuh), I do not know if Jesus said this or not, but that is irrelevant to the point. The Prophet loved children. He would laugh with them and give them sweets. He would always show them affection and mercy. Once a man came to him and said, "I have ten children and have never kissed any of them." The Prophet cast a look at him and said, *"Whoever is not merciful to others will not be treated mercifully."* You are correct that every culture values and protects its children. You are wrong that "it is not a cultural practice for us as it is in some Islamic countries." What are the Catholic Church scandals all about? There are bad people in every religion and in every country. We do not blame a culture or country for heinous crimes like this; we blame the individual.

Finally, regarding why we live like we did 2000 years ago, I think you have confused your history. 2000 years ago is the age when Jesus (pbuh) was preaching; 1500 years ago is the age when Muhammad (pbuh) was born. At that time, Europe was in its

Dark Ages and Arabia was an insignificant suburb of the Persian and Byzantine empires. Fast-forward to a hundred years after the Prophet's death and you have a blossoming civilization that was the leader of the arts, sciences, and technology.

Jared Diamond, a world-renowned UCLA sociologist and physiologist, won the Pulitzer Prize for his book, **Guns, Germs, and Steel**, in which he wrote: *"Medieval Islam was technologically advanced and open to innovation. It achieved far higher literacy rates than in contemporary Europe; it assimilated the legacy of classical Greek civilization to such a degree that many classical books are now known to us only through Arabic copies. It invented windmills, trigonometry, lateen sails and made major advances in metallurgy, mechanical and chemical engineering and irrigation methods. In the middle-ages the flow of technology was overwhelmingly from Islam to Europe rather from Europe to Islam. Only after the 1500's did the net direction of flow begin to reverse."* (pg. 253)

You can also check out this link:
http://en.wikipedia.org/wiki/Islamic_Golden_Age

Islam was the reason for this Enlightenment. It wasn't until Muslims abandoned the teachings of Islam that backwardness emerged and took root in Muslim societies, as you see today.

5. Regardless of theological interpretations, it is acknowledged by both Catholic and Protestant churches that a woman covering her hair signified modesty, chastity, and piety. This is why almost every picture of Mary, mother of Jesus (peace be upon them) shows her with hair covered.

As for your second comment, no, it is not accurate. Women cover themselves to obey God's guidance to achieve modesty, chastity, and piety. The 'protection' you speak of is a side-benefit, not the ultimate reason.

The Qur'an says: **Tell believing men to lower their gaze and remain chaste. That is purer for them. God is aware of what they do. Say to believing women that they should lower their gaze and remain chaste and not to reveal their adornments—save what is normally apparent thereof, and they should fold their shawls over their bosoms. They can only reveal their**

adornments to their husbands or their fathers... (24:30-31)

The verse goes on to list the people who are allowed to see a Muslim woman's adornments or beauty. The list is basically the woman's male relatives, female friends, and small children.

The first point we see is that men are ordered to lower their gaze, so those "unclean eyes" are sinning against the command of God. The second point is that women are commanded to hide their beauty when around men who are not related or married to her. The hijab is not an emblem of female servitude; that's a Christian concept:

http://www.bibleviews.com/Veil.html

In Islam, it is an emblem of modesty and piety before God Almighty. It can be interpreted as a feminist statement: "My body is not for public consumption; it is only for the man that *I* choose to be my husband to enjoy."

6. You bring up many points here. We addressed the covering of feminine beauty above. Basically, the woman's beauty is **reserved** for the man she *chooses* to take as a husband. This empowers her to be treated as a dignified human being, not a sex object. Sexual attractiveness is for her husband's eyes only.

As for female circumcision, this is a practice that was around in Arabia before the birth of the Prophet. Since the Arabs back then would just remove the tip of the clitoral hood, the male and female circumcisions were really almost identical. Islam came and confirmed that male circumcision is mandatory but stated that female circumcision was merely permissible. Women could either get the operation or not. Islam does not prescribe, nor does it condone the mutilation and removal of the female genitals. The Prophet said that a woman has a **right** to sexual satisfaction, so how could Islam infringe on that God-given right?

Your questions about women remind me of the story of Yvonne Ridley. She was the journalist captured by the Taliban while reporting undercover in Afghanistan, soon after 9/11. Held on spying charges, she feared she would be stoned. Instead, she was treated with respect. She promised her captors that after her release she would study Islam.

She read the Qur'an, looking for an **explanation** of the Taliban's treatment of women, *only to find there wasn't any.* As she saw it, "It's a magna carta for women!" She converted in the summer of 2003 and has found that her new faith has helped put behind her three broken marriages and her drinking problem.

Again, I apologize for the length of the email, but I wanted to be sure each point was addressed as fully as possible.

I look forward to your response.

May peace be with you,

Ahmed

Email #06 – From: Jessica
Sent: Saturday, March 27, 2010 1:34 p.m.
To: Ahmed Rashed

Thank you for your response. Do not apologize that it is too long; I enjoy reading. It would seem that it is Man who corrupts religion for his own reasons of power or to subjugate and not what God teaches. I acknowledge that this has also been true of Catholic and Protestant religions throughout history. However, with all the media controversy on the varying ways that Islam is practiced throughout the world it is hard to understand without the knowledge of the Qur'an that you have passed on. For that I thank you. I like to think of myself as a very accepting person of people who are different and take a live and let live approach until it interferes with what I consider fundamental rights that every human should have; to live in peace, to be treated with honour and respect and for the least of our society to be protected and safe.

I am familiar with the captured reporter that you speak of; Yvonne Ridley. I also understand that there are very good and respectful people in your society and I take no pleasure in the life of fear and uncertainty that the children of Iraq and Afghanistan are enduring under wars that if I don't understand, I can't imagine they could. I simply understand from our Canadian perspective that the overthrow of the Taliban was necessary for a stable future, I pray peace will eventually come for the people of Afghanistan.

Unfortunately, in a day in which 100% of all terrorists acts against our society are perpetrated 100% by extremists for whatever reasons, we can fathom you have a very difficult job of educating the public.

Email #07 – From: Ahmed Rashed
Sent: Wednesday, March 31, 2010 10:55 p.m.
To: Jessica

In the Name of God, the Most-Gracious, the Ever-Merciful:
I am glad you were able to benefit from our conversation. It takes patience and a willingness to understand to cut through the media sensationalism and dogma. For that, I thank you for asking, and I thank you for listening.

If you ever have any other questions about Islam or Muslims, please feel free to email me again.

May peace be with you,
Ahmed

CONVERSATION WITH BERNIE

Islamic Worship, Prayer, Charity, and Pilgrimage

Email #02 – From: Bernie
Sent: Monday, March 29, 2010 8:49 p.m.
To: Ahmed Rashed

Mr. Rashed,
I received an English translated copy of the Qur'an today. I've even begun to peruse it. I am humored by the fact that although this is a translation, it by no means conveys the message written. I have both read and been told that in order to truly understand the Qur'an, one must learn the language. Alas, my language skills are severely lacking. As a natural skeptic, I believe that the Bible, the Qur'an, or any "religious tome" is merely a book written by man. Perhaps, men that thought they were inspired by some higher deity, however men none the less. And like the days of old, men still twist words to fit ideas and beliefs. My experience with multiple facets of Christianity have led me to my current skepticism and in this my current distrust of all modern religions. I consider all religions born around the time of Christ to be "modern." For many years in my late teens and early twenties, I sought the right religion. Alas, I never found what I searched for. My beliefs are founded on my experiences. I base no assessment on media or others perceived notion of what is or is not. Clearly, I am curious enough about Islam to submit to correspondence otherwise I would have not written my first message. In point of fact, that which brought me down this road is my love of music or more specifically recent research of bands/musicians (Outlandish) with Islamic beliefs. Is this the path I will take? Perhaps, God, Allah, whatever title we give him knows.

What Would a Muslim Say?

Email #03 – From: Ahmed Rashed
Sent: Thursday, April 1, 2010 1:20 p.m.
To: Bernie

In the Name of God, the Most-Gracious, the Ever-Merciful:
Regarding the Qur'an being in Arabic, God has always revealed His Scriptures in the language of the people that received it. So the Torah was revealed in Hebrew, the Evangel was revealed in Aramaic, and the Qur'an was revealed in Arabic. This is so the prophet and his community could directly understand the message. The Final Testament is in Arabic, but that does not mean that Arabs are a "chosen people," for it is a fact that less than 20% of today's Muslims are Arabs.

The Qur'an came primarily to deliver a Message to humanity, and this Message can be translated and understood into all languages. For this reason, we see many converts from Greek, Egyptian, and Persian backgrounds in the early history of Islam. However, only the meaning of the message of the Qur'an can be translated, not the Qur'an itself; so all translations have always been seen as approximations or interpretations. It is precisely because of this firm stance that the Qur'an has been preserved for over fourteen centuries without any changes. The Arabic language never died away or changed irrevocably, because Muslims (Arab and non-Arab) had to recite the Qur'an in Arabic for their mandatory prayers.

The obligatory prayers must be said in Arabic so as to bring unity to the Muslim community, not to impose any hardship. The idea is that any Muslim, no matter where he is from, can read and pray the same way as every other Muslim in the world and feel that he is truly a part of a single brotherhood.

May peace be with you,
Ahmed

Email #04 – From: Bernie
Sent: Thursday, April 1, 2010 9:30 p.m.
To: Ahmed Rashed

Mr. Rashed,

Christians, Jews, and Muslims all pray to the same God. Yet year after year there is war and strife based on whose belief is the right one.

Why prayer five times a day? What is the significance? Of the tithe paid, how much goes to organizational overhead and how much actually gets to where it is needed most? Who decides where the funding goes? It irritates me to see High Office persons of any faith, for that matter any organization, get the best luxuries while those they supposedly support don't get but a fraction of what was donated. Other than I like to travel, why must one make a pilgrimage to Mecca?

I imagine, as I read the Qur'an and listen to it spoken as I read it, I will have more questions. I am humored now. My aunt was until now a devout Christian. Now, she has accepted Judaism in her life through her best friend. I talked to her about my exploring Islam yesterday. She was vehemently against my exploration, even after she's known the challenges I've faced. People tend to be closed-minded, especially when the topic is outside their realm of understanding. Lately I've been sampling Islamic Pop and Nasheed music. Today the music initiated conversation from multiple people. There were some good but mostly biased opinions. I cannot believe I am actually playing devil's advocate when my coworkers base their assessments and beliefs on others speculations and biases. Well, alas I must retire. I have to be at work in six hours.

Respectfully,
Bernie

Email #05 – From: Ahmed Rashed
Sent: Sunday, April 4, 2010 2:35 p.m.
To: Bernie

In the Name of God, the Most-Gracious, the Ever-Merciful:
The war and strife is not based on whose belief is the right one. Every war has been over land or resources. God alone will judge mankind on Judgment Day.

The Qur'an says:

There is no compulsion in religion. (2:256)

Had your Lord willed, everyone on earth would have believed. Will you compel people to become believers? (10:99)

And say, "The truth is from your Lord. Whoever wills — let him believe. And whoever wills — let him disbelieve." (18:29)

Regarding the prayer, the Arabic word for Prayer — *Salat* — comes from the root **ta-si-la,** which means "connected." So the daily prayers are seen as the direct connection between the Creator and those devoted to the Creator. The Qur'an says: **Recite what is revealed to you of the Book and establish the Prayer. Verily Prayer restrains from immorality and injustice; and truly the remembrance of God is greater. And God knows what you do. (29:45)**

The Prophet said: *"If there was a river at the door of anyone of you and he took a bath in it five times a day, would you notice any dirt on him?" They said, "Not a trace of dirt would be left." The Prophet continued, "That is the example of the five prayers with which God blots out evil deeds."*

As for the "tithe," zakah is usually given directly from the donor to the needy. Zakah may be distributed directly to individuals of one or more of the eligible categories, or to welfare organizations that look after them. Muslims usually research organizations before giving them anything so they are satisfied with how much of their donations get to the recipients.

Historically, the local governor of an Islamic city/province would collect all the zakah from his constituency and then distribute it to the eligibles in his area. If there was surplus after distribution, the surplus was sent to the central ruler for redistribution in other provinces. If there was shortage after distribution, a letter was sent to central ruler requesting the amount needed to cover shortage. In this way, richer provinces helped poorer provinces.

There are eight categories of recipients explicitly spelled out in the Qur'an (9:60):

1. The poor Muslims, to relieve their distress; 2. The needy Muslims to supply them with means for their livelihood; 3. The new Muslim converts, to enable them to settle down and meet their unusual needs; 4. The Muslim prisoners of war, to liberate them by payment of ransom money; 5. The Muslims and non-Muslims in debt, to free them from their liabilities incurred under pressing necessities; 6. The Muslim employees appointed by a Muslim governor for the collection of zakah to pay their wages (tradition dictates that total payment to zakah collectors cannot exceed 1/8th [12.5%] of total amount collected collections); 7. The Muslims in service of the cause of God by means of research or study or propagation of Islam. This share is to cover their expenses and help them to continue their services; 8. The Muslim wayfarers who are stranded in a foreign land and in need of help.

There are no "high offices" in Islam. Your irritation is justified; it is for this reason that Islam does not recognize any offices. Every person stands before God on his own faith and deeds. As the late scholar, al-Mawdudi, summarized the Prophet's teachings, *"You are human beings and all human beings are equal in the eyes of God. Distinctions of birth and race are no criteria of greatness and nobility. Devotion to God and service to humanity are the standards by which God will judge. There is an appointed day after your death when you shall have to appear before your Lord. You shall be called to account for all your deeds, and you shall not be able then to hide anything. Your fate shall be determined by your good or bad actions. True faith and good deeds alone will stand you in good stead at that time. He who has them shall take his abode in the Heaven of eternal happiness, while he who is devoid of them shall be cast in the fire of Hell."*

What Would a Muslim Say?

As for why Muslims make the pilgrimage, it is the last communal obligation that was revealed to the Prophet. Mecca marks the spot where the Prophet Abraham first built a shrine to worship God. It was a caravan crossroads through rocky outcroppings in the desert, which grew into a modern, noisy, bustling center.

The Qur'an says: **Say: 'God has spoken the truth; therefore follow the creed of Abraham, a man of pure faith and no idolater.' The first House established for the people was that at Bekka, a place holy, and guidance to all beings. Therein are clear signs — the station of Abraham, and whosoever enters it is in security. It is the duty of all men towards God to come to the House a pilgrim, if he is able to make his way there. As for the unbeliever, God is All-sufficient nor needs any being. (3:95-97)**

The Qur'an says the Pilgrimage started with Abraham: **We showed Abraham the location of the House: "Do not associate anything with Me; and purify My House for those who circle around, and those who stand to pray, and those who kneel and prostrate." And announce the pilgrimage to humanity. They will come to you on foot, and on every transport. They will come from every distant point.**

That they may witness the benefits for themselves, and celebrate the name of God during the appointed days, for providing them with the animal livestock. So eat from it, and feed the unfortunate poor.

Then let them perform their acts of cleansing, and fulfill their vows, and circle around the Ancient House. All that. Whoever venerates the sanctities of God — it is good for him with his Lord. All livestock are permitted to you, except what is recited to you. So stay away from the abomination of idols, and stay away from perjury. (22:26-30)

So Muslims are commemorating Abraham's covenant with God and retrace the steps of Abraham, his wife Hajar, and his son Ishmael. This symbolizes the continuation of the Message that God gave to Abraham and all the prophets after him, regardless of race, nationality, language, or color.

I pray that I can continue to be of service to you as you continue your exploration. Feel free to ask me anything about what you've read or if a coworker asked you something you did not know how to answer.

May peace be with you,
Ahmed

CONVERSATION WITH SATISH

Salvation and Tolerance in Islam

Email #02 – From: Ahmed Rashed
Sent: Wednesday, April 7, 2010 1:58 a.m.
To: Satish

Dear Sir,

It is very clear that the Qur'an gives sanction to fight by saying 'cause of God.' It is clear it is the God of Islam, not others. Others are 'Kafeers.' So let us not try to overlook the present situation.

Email #03 – From: Ahmed Rashed
Sent: Wednesday, April 7, 2010 11:15 a.m.
To: Satish

In the Name of God, the Most-Gracious, the Ever-Merciful:

I pray this email finds you in the best of health and faith, God-willing. "Fighting in God's cause" is the most misunderstood concept in our faith.

The word "jihad" comes from the root word **ja-ha-da**, which means to struggle. At the individual level, jihad primarily refers to the inner struggle of being a person of virtue and submission to God in all aspects of life. It does not mean "holy war." Jihad on the battlefield, in the Islamic perspective, is the last resort, and is subject to stringent conditions. It can be waged only to defend freedom, which includes freedom of faith.

Please reply back at your earliest convenience so we may continue the discussion, for it is only through dialogue that we can attain understanding.

May peace be with you,
Ahmed Rashed

Email #04 – From: Satish
Sent: Thursday, April 8, 2010 4:43 a.m.
To: Ahmed Rashed

Dear Mr. Rashed,

Thank you very much for reply. Can I know how 'Kafeer' is defined in Islam?

Satish

Email #05 – From: Ahmed Rashed
Sent: Saturday, April 10, 2010 5:14 p.m.
To: Satish

In the Name of God, the Most-Gracious, the Ever-Merciful:

There is no word "kafeer" in Arabic. There is the root word, "**ka-fa-ra**" which means to reject, refuse, remove, hide, or deny. From this word, the Qur'an conjugates the root in many ways to get various meanings.

A few of the more common meanings are:

1. **Kaafir**: disbeliever — literally a rejector of faith; opposite of believer.

2. **Kafoor**: ingrate — literally one who refuses to thank; opposite of thankful.

3. **Kaf-fir**: expiate — literally renounce; usually used to describe how God expiates (completely removes) the sins of those who repent.

4. **Yakfir**: cover — literally hide; used in a few verses to describe hypocrites (they hide/cover their true feelings).

In Islamic Studies, the first and second meanings are used most. So **Kaafir** (disbeliever) is the opposite of **Mu'min** (believer), and **Kafoor** (ingrate) is the opposite of **Shakoor** (thankful).

Getting back to your original point, however, is the understanding that Muslims worship the same One God that the other monotheistic faiths revere. The Qur'an says: **Say: We believe in that which has been revealed to us and revealed to you. Our God and your God is one. And to Him we surrender ourselves. (29:46)**

So to say "it is the God of Islam, not others" is not quite accurate. It is written in the Qur'an that God sent prophets to each nation in history. In other words, God made a covenant with every people in every time. This covenant was "*Islam,*" which means surrender and obedience to God, and a person who surrenders his will to God and obeys His commandments is called a "*Muslim.*" Those who disobey God or reject any one of His prophets is called a "**Kafir**" or "Rejector."

I pray this email answered your question and addressed your concerns. Anything beneficial is from God; any mistakes or harm is from my own shortcomings.

May peace be with you,

Ahmed

Email #06 – From: Satish
Sent: Sunday, April 11, 2010 1:44 a.m.
To: Ahmed Rashed

Dear Mr. Rashed,

Thank you very much for your explanation. What happens to people who do not believe in God? They may be Kafeers. But they are human beings. Some of them are great human beings like Albert Einstein. Does Islam have space for such nonbelievers, or do they have no right to live their lives?

Further, the Hindu faith talks of one God at the highest level. However, at levels lower than the highest there are different manifestation of God accepted as a part of overall Hindu faith. Hindus not only accept believers but also atheists. I don't know if the concept of *Vasudaivakutumbakam* exists. This means "earth is one family." Acceptance of others' faith without reservation is part of the Hindu method. When Arabs came to Kerala they were given land to build a mosque. I would like to know if nonbelievers are accepted in Islam.

Satish

Email #07 – From: Ahmed Rashed
Sent: Wednesday, April 14, 2010 12:07 p.m.
To: Satish

Islamic doctrine holds that human existence continues after the death of the human body in the form of spiritual and physical resurrection. There is a direct relation between conduct on earth and the life beyond. The afterlife will be one of rewards and punishments which are commensurate with earthly conduct. A day will come when God will resurrect and gather the first and the last of His creation and judge everyone justly. People will enter their final abode, Hell or Paradise. Faith in life after death urges us to do right and to stay away from sin. In this life we sometimes see the pious suffer and the impious prosper. All shall be judged one day and justice will be served.

On the Last Day, resurrected humans and Jinn will be judged by Allah according to their deeds. One's eternal destination depends primarily on correct belief, and secondarily on balance of good to bad deeds in life. They are either granted admission to Paradise, where they will enjoy spiritual and physical pleasures forever, or condemned to Hell to suffer spiritual and physical torment for eternity.

Paradise is for those who worshipped God alone, believed and followed their prophet, **and** lived moral lives according to the teachings of scripture.

Hell will be the final dwelling place of those who denied God, worshipped other beings besides God, rejected the call of the prophets, **or** led sinful, unrepentant lives.

This is because the Qur'an tells us that the whole REASON why God created people on this Earth was so they could know God. This worldly life is just a test to see who would seek to know God, and from this knowledge, love, worship, and obey Him. Therefore, a person who denies God or refuses to worship Him as He has commanded has failed to fulfill his purpose of existence.

On the other hand, a person who denies God still has all the rights to life, wealth, family, honor, and mind like a Muslim.

These are fundamental human rights in Islamic law, regardless of whether a human being believes or disbelieves. So a disbeliever has the right to "live their lives" as you said, but Islam teaches that the **final** state of such a person is not the same as one who believes.

May peace be with you,
Ahmed

Email #08 – From: Satish
Sent: Thursday, April 15, 2010 12:36 a.m.
To: Ahmed Rashed

Dear Mr. Rashed,

I think that there is a miscommunication. I was not talking of afterlife. I wanted to know as to how Islam views people who are nonbelievers of God, worshippers of Idols, trees, etc. **in this life**. Are they considered as Kafeers and hence are subject to jihad?

Satish

Email #09 – From: Ahmed Rashed
Sent: Sunday, April 18, 2010 6:39 a.m.
To: Satish

In the Name of God, the Most-Gracious, the Ever-Merciful

As I wrote in my previous email, a person who denies God still has all the rights to life, wealth, family, honor, and intellect that a Muslim has. These are fundamental human rights in Islamic law, regardless of whether a human being believes or disbelieves.

Islam does **not** condone the killing of innocent people. The Prophet said the following:

"Whoever hurts a non-Muslim citizen of a Muslim state has hurt me, and he who hurts me has offended God."

"He who hurts a non-Muslim citizen of a Muslim state, I am his adversary; and I shall be his adversary on the Day of Judgment."

*"Anyone who kills a non-Muslim who had a pact of peace with us will **not** smell the fragrance of Paradise."*

What Would a Muslim Say?

From this, Islamic scholars are unanimous that the life, property, and honor of non-Muslims who do not attack Muslims or drive them from their homes are as sacred as the life, property, and honor of Muslims.

So in conclusion, fighting and waging war is only allowed to defend faith, life, and homeland. It is only lawful and justified to stop aggression, persecution, or injustice.

May peace be with you,

Ahmed

Email #10 – From: Satish
Sent: Sunday, April 18, 2010 9:24 a.m.
To: Ahmed Rashed

Dear Mr. Rashed,

Thanks for you clarification. Good to know properly. Unfortunate, wrong interpretations are made in the name of Islam. It has been very useful for me.

Satish

Email #11 – From: Ahmed Rashed
Sent: Sunday, April 18, 2010 11:01 a.m.
To: Satish

Dear Satish,

You are quite welcome. This is the reason why we made the WhyIslam website. There is so much wrong understanding and propaganda in the media, we felt it necessary to make a site to give authentic information about Islam.

I hope you will feel free to ask me any other questions about Islam that you may have in the future.

May peace be with you,

Ahmed

With Dialogue Comes Understanding

CONVERSATION WITH WITH JESSICA - PART 2

Muslim Culture and Modernity

**Email #01 – From: Jessica
Sent: Wednesday, July 28, 2010 12:37 a.m.
To: Ahmed Rashed**

It takes a Brit to put into words what we should be saying. Wow, this is good. https://www.jihadwatch.org/2010/06/pat-condell-on-ground-zero-mosque-is-it-possible-to-be-astonished-but-not-surprised. Condell is a British stand-up comedian, but this video isn't comic, it's pure truth, and utterly brilliant.

**Email #02 – From: Ahmed Rashed
Sent: Thursday, July 29, 2010 9:19 a.m.
To: Jessica**

Hello Jessica,
I received this email and the other one called "The Real Truth" with Geert Wilder's speech. I also see that you tried to recall both emails. The contents of the emails are very strong and emotional, if not quite accurate. Would you like to have a conversation about them? After our last exchange of emails, it seems good to address the issues in these emails.
May peace be with you,
Ahmed Rashed

**Email #03 – From: Jessica
Sent: Thursday, July 29, 2010 6:11 p.m.
To: Ahmed Rashed**

You are right; I attempted to recall them because they are only opinions, all of which I am sure you are aware of. I should have also attached an explanation of why I would have sent them in the first place and that would have been to express the fears and the concerns of a very different culture living amongst us; but these would also not be new to you either.

I guess ultimately history will tell the outcome of the two very different cultures. I would hate to think of Europe or the Americas losing our own culture in the process.

Email #04 – From: Ahmed Rashed
Sent: Friday, July 30, 2010 1:51 p.m.
To: Jessica

In the Name of God, the Most-Gracious, the Ever-Merciful:
These opinions, as I said in my first email, are not based on facts. Rather they are based on fear and ignorance. The majority of Muslims do not have any agenda for world domination. While there are aspects of American and European culture that are distasteful to Islamic morals and societal norms, the Qur'an is very clear: **There is no compulsion in faith. (2:256)**

A Muslim or group of Muslims are religiously required to speak out against injustices and/or immorality they see in society, but they do not have the permission to take the law into their own hands to stop these injustices or immorality. A Muslim is bound to admonish or advise the people around him if he sees them going against the Divine Guidance of the Qur'an and Prophetic teachings, but in the end, people are free to accept the advice or ignore it.

It should be clearly understood that the mission of Prophet Muhammad (peace be on him) was not political, social, or economic reform, although such reforms were a logical consequence of the success of this mission. His mission was not the unity of a nation and the establishment of an empire, although the nation did unite and vast areas came under one administration. His mission was not the spread of a civilization or culture, although many civilizations and cultures developed. Rather, his mission was **only to deliver the message of God to all the peoples of the world and to invite them to submit to Him, while being the foremost among those who submitted.**

So once the message has been delivered, the responsibility of the Muslim ends, and any further action is a TRANSGRESSION against the very same Laws of God that the Muslim claims to be advocating. As a famous scholar once said, "You cannot break the Law in order to implement the Law."

So every single example that Mr. Wilders uses to highlight Muslim intolerance is in fact a transgression against the means and ends that Islam calls for.

The Qur'an is very clear:

Had your Lord willed, everyone on earth would have believed. Will you compel people to become believers? (10:99)

And say, "The truth is from your Lord. Whoever wills — let him believe. And whoever wills — let him disbelieve." (18:29)

... And thou are not a guardian over them. (Multiple)

That last phrase is repeated often and in multiple places in the Qur'an. Just as the Prophet was only charged with delivering the message and inviting all to it, Muslims are only charged with delivering the message and inviting all to it. Whoever rejects the invitation is left alone so long as he doesn't start fighting Muslims because of their religion or driving Muslims out of their homes. We talked about this during our last email exchange (see Qur'an 60:6-8).

For over a thousand years, Muslim minorities in non-Muslim majorities (see the history of China, Indonesia, the Philippines, and sub-Saharan Africa) behaved according to this. For over a thousand years, Muslim majorities treated their non-Muslim minorities with justice unheard of in those times. Bad Muslims are bad Muslims; therefore, the problem is not Islam, but the people who are failing to live up to the ideals of Islam.

As for the Ground Zero Mosque, if the perpetrators were Muslim, but every major Islamic organization, scholar, and advocacy group has condemned the attacks as un-Islamic, then obviously those attacks are NOT the product of mainstream Islam. So what is the problem with having a cultural center (of which only part is a mosque) there to teach the correct understanding of Islam for both non-Muslims and Muslims?

May peace be with you,

Ahmed

Email #05 – From: Jessica
Sent: Friday, July 30, 2010 11:56 p.m.
To: Ahmed Rashed

Well, there are aspects of the Muslim culture that are very distasteful to those of Western culture as well. That is obviously what we fear.

So apparently living as we do in the West is immoral, but stoning someone or convincing martyrs to blow themselves up is not. Muhammad is okay with that? Freedom, I think, is what our Western Culture (Europe & America) is based on.

I am sorry, but you cannot deny the attack on the World Trade Center was done by Islamic (Muslim) extremists. This may not be, as you say, the norm. However, do you not think that the vast majority of Muslim cultures are extreme? You speak of the tolerance to minority non-Muslims. Would that be like the British couple who were kissing on the beach and condemned in a Saudi court? Again, religion and politics should never mix.

Jesus was the only true prophet and the son of God. He was loving, accepting, and gave people "choice." Our Christian faith is all about "choice." I see no Islamic culture that truly gives people choice. Daughters are condemned if they do not "cover" themselves. I am sorry; did God make something that is not good?

Email #06 – From: Ahmed Rashed
Sent: Thursday, August 5, 2010 1:52 a.m.
To: Jessica

In the Name of God, the Most-Gracious, the Ever-Merciful:

Dear Jessica,

I pray this email finds you in the best of health and faith, God-willing. I apologize for my delay in responding to you. I was out of town this weekend, so I didn't see your email until I returned. You brought up many points, so it took me some time to write a response. I am also in the process of responding to your other email with the CNN article.

I will address your concerns point by point, God-willing. Again, I ask you to forgive me for the length of this email.

Well; there are aspects of the Muslim culture that are very distasteful to those of Western culture as well. That is obviously what we fear.

What is this distaste based on? Is it based on the actions of Muslims or the basic teachings of Islam? As I have been trying to explain since we first started corresponding, there is a difference between Muslim culture and Islamic culture. The first is what Muslims are doing; the second is what Muslims SHOULD be doing. With very few exceptions, Muslims are not living up to the ideals, principles, or values of Islam.

The principles and values of Islam have historically been praised by non-Muslims because of its wisdom, justice, practicality, and universalism. Why else is Islam growing so fast among Western men and women? Why is the conversion rate among Western **women** greater than that of men? Do they not think like you think? Do they not read the newspapers like you do? Do they not see what is going on in the world like you see? Of course not; the difference is they look beyond the actions of imperfect human beings and look to the teachings of the Qur'an and the Prophet and find in it wisdom, light, and guidance.

So apparently living as we do in the West is immoral

The current Western lifestyle is not only considered immoral in the opinion of Muslims. It is also the opinion of devout Christians. Check out this link:

http://www.chapellibrary.org/pdf-english/cmod.pdf

But stoning someone or convincing martyrs to blow themselves up is not. Muhammad is okay with that?

Stoning is the divinely prescribed punishment for the sin and crime of adultery in ALL three Abrahamic faiths: Judaism, Christianity, and Islam. There are very strong conditions that MUST BE MET before such a conviction can be made or carried out in Islam. I will explain these conditions in the second email that deals specifically with the CNN article you sent me.

As for "convincing martyrs to blow themselves up," I have **already** told you in the previous exchange of emails that these acts are *against* the mainstream teachings of Islam. Suicide is absolutely forbidden; the Prophet said that the man who purposefully takes his own life will automatically go to Hell and never see Paradise (see also the Qur'an 4:29-30). Killing noncombatants is absolutely forbidden; the Prophet repeatedly instructed his companions that the children, the women, the elderly, the farmer in the field, the craftsman in his shop, the laborers, and those who surrender SHOULD NOT BE HARMED. I think this is very clear evidence that Muhammad (peace be upon him) would **not** be okay with that. And there are scholars and sheikhs around the world who say the same. See in the link below:

http://www.muhajabah.com/otherscondemn.php

Freedom, I think, that is what our Western Culture (Europe & America) is based on.

No, that is not true. Modern Western culture is based on SECULAR HUMANISM. Freedom is merely a temporary byproduct of focusing on individual humanism as opposed to societal humanism. We know this because personal freedom was routinely bypassed or trampled by secular humanistic societies in their goal for satisfying whatever their desires were at the moment. The 20th century is filled with examples of this.

This worldview came about as a result of Western men's disillusionment with the church. Historically, during Renaissance times, the word emphasized the importance of man, not to the exclusion of God, but simply with little emphasis on God. Today this view holds that man is the ultimate standard by which all life is measured and judged. Thus, we find that values, law, justice, good, beauty, and right-and-wrong are to be judged by man-made rules with no credence to either God or the Scriptures.

The humanist believes that man will be able to solve all his own problems and that "man is the measure of all things." In today's world, humanism is quite popular, even with people who claim to be religious (Jewish, Christian, and Muslim).

This is why Muslims seem so exotic and strange to the Western man. The observant Muslim (like the observant Christian and Jew) still believes in higher truths. He still believes there is an absolute standard of right and wrong that does not change with time or place. There are *many* devout Christians and devout Jews who are aghast at the immorality and injustice running rampant in our world today. This is why Muslims speak out and lobby and argue and try to change the corrupt status quo. The Prophet said, *"He who sees evil should stop it with his hand. If he does not have the power, then he should speak out against it with his tongue. If he does not have the power to do that, then he should dislike it in his heart; and that is the weakest level of faith."*

Islam never claimed that individual freedom is the highest value in the society. In fact, Islam claims the morality of the society is more important than individual freedom. This claim is supported by the fact that unrestrained individual freedom leads to an immoral and fragmented society that is prone to injustices. It is **societal** morality and justice that drives Islamic culture. Muslims are not perfect, but it is this societal perfection that we pursue. If a person wants to sin in the privacy of their own home, Islam says they are free to do so. No Muslim can violate his right to privacy; God will judge them on the Last Day. However, Islam teaches that blatant and brazen violations of <u>public</u> morality should be censured. It is by upholding this public morality that Islam intends to reform and uplift society.

I am sorry, but you cannot deny the attack on the World Trade Center was done by Islamic (Muslim) extremists.

I never denied that Muslim extremists committed those attacks. I simply said, like all other mainstream Islamic leaders and organizations, that these attacks are against the values and principles of Islam:

http://www.religioustolerance.org/islfatwa.htm

What Would a Muslim Say?

This may not be, as you say, the norm. However, do you not think that the vast majority of Muslim cultures are extreme?

What "vast majority" are you talking about? Really, do you think there would be any stable societies anywhere in Muslim-majority countries if the vast majority of Muslims were as you imagine? It is not. These same extreme actions which are done by a minority are denounced by me and all those Muslims who have studied the Qur'an and the Prophet. This is not just Muslims living in the West. This is Yemen, Saudi Arabia, Egypt, Pakistan, Indonesia, and Turkey (to name a few). In case you've failed to notice, the majority of the victims of 'terrorist bombings' since 9/11 have been Muslims.

Have you listened to what Muslim preachers are actually preaching? Here is one English Islamic Channel:

http://www.watchislam.com/tv1/

Listen to a few programs, and you will see they say the same thing that I am saying now. Muslims have gone astray. We have left the spirit of our religious teachings. We have become so concerned with the *letter* of the texts that we have forgotten the *spirit* behind the texts. The point is this: **The extremism of Muslim culture is a result of <u>leaving</u> the values and principles of Islam, not a result of <u>following</u> them.**

You speak of the tolerance to minority non-Muslims. Would that be like the British couple who were kissing on the beach and condemned in a Saudi court?

First of all, I searched Google, Bing, and Yahoo for this. I found a story about a British couple having sex on a Dubai beach. I found a story about a British couple kissing in a Dubai restaurant. Perhaps you were referring to one of these reports.

In regard to the first story, your objections are somewhat hypocritical. An American couple on a public American beach would have similarly been arrested and convicted of public indecency. The only difference is that comparable American convictions have resulted in thirty to forty days in county jail instead of three months as was done in Dubai.

In regard to the second story, the verdict is still pending, and the only reason that this was even brought to court was because there were children witnesses. Even in the USA, if an act of public sexual affection is done in front of a child, the guardians of that child usually file a complaint to the police. This case is only different in that most devout Muslims are very sensitive to their children being exposed to public displays of sexual affection.

I fail to see how either of these incidents shows lack of tolerance from Muslims to non-Muslim minorities.

Again, religion and politics should never mix.

This is exactly the calling card of secular humanism. This is a fragmented worldview. It is this idea is that leads men to sing hymns on Sunday and commit sins on Monday. I know pastors who preach against this in their sermons, so what is the difference if Muslims try to adhere to the same standards all week? When a human being is taught to disassociate his faith, beliefs, and ethics from his day-to-day life, you get financial corruption, marital infidelity, road rage, and the like. Islam teaches that all spheres of human activity can and should be guided by Divine Wisdom. That is the purpose of God sending Scripture down to the Messengers: to give His creatures a roadmap to achieving piety and God-consciousness in all that they do.

Jesus was the only true prophet and the son of God. He was loving, accepting, and gave people "choice."

Muslims do not believe Jesus claimed to be the son of God. Muslims do not see themselves as choosing Muhammad over Jesus (peace be upon them both). Rather, the message of Muhammad revives the original teachings of Jesus (peace be upon him) and all the Prophets before him and corrects all the man-made additions that crept into the original teachings of Jesus (peace be upon him).

That is why it says in the Qur'an: **O People of the Scripture! Do not exaggerate in your religion, and do not say about God except the truth. The Messiah, Jesus, the son of Mary,** is the Messenger of God, and His Word that He conveyed to Mary, and a Spirit from Him. So believe in God and His messengers, and do not say, "Three." Refrain — it is better for you. God is only one God. Glory be to Him — that He should have a son. To Him belongs everything in the heavens and the earth, and God is a sufficient Protector. (4:171)

Our Christian faith is all about "choice." I see no Islamic culture that truly gives people choice.

I think that most Christians feel that their own religion should not be "a la carte," so why is it so hard to understand that Muslims feel the same way? As I pointed out before, there is no compulsion for non-Muslims to become Muslim, so there is a choice. However, once a person makes that choice — the choice to submit their will to God and to devote their lives to God's service — he or she must live by the principles that God dictates. It means I have to worship God on HIS terms, not my terms. It isn't really devotion if I pick and choose which parts of God's revelations I want to observe. I think that even a Christian would call someone who picks and chooses a hypocrite.

Daughters are condemned if they do not "cover" themselves.

Again, do you really think this is true? There are hundreds of millions of Muslim women out there that do not "cover" themselves, yet you don't see any systematic, Islam-inspired condemnation or harassment or killing of them, do you? No, those killings and harassments are the product of a few Muslims that go to extremes. *Islam does not teach this.* Muslim preachers and scholars do preach about modesty and how such actions are sinful, but they do not call for killing them or anything of the sort.

After the Prophet Muhammad (peace be upon him) died, his young widow Aisha saw some women visit Medina. She asked them, "Who are you?" They said, "We are the women from Syria." She said, "If you are believers, then know that this is not the dress of a believing woman. But if you are not believers, then enjoy this worldly life." This is how she dealt with Muslim women who didn't adhere to the Islamic dress code. No vindications. No calls for honor killings. No repelling. Just a reminder of how a believing woman is supposed to appear in public.

Three of my four female cousins do not wear hijab. They live in Egypt. They're doing fine, and no one harasses or tries to kill them. A friend of mine is married to a woman who does not wear hijab. They are from Pakistan. Both them have women in their family still in Pakistan who do not wear hijab. They are also living without fear of killings of condemnation. They get occasional reminders from religious family members and friends, but that's it. You describe isolated events, not general action.

I am sorry; did God make something that is not good?

Ask the Catholic nun if wearing her habit means God made something that is not good. Ask the Amish, Anabaptist, and Methodist woman if covering her hair means God made something that is not good. After you hear their answers, go ask a Muslim woman if covering her body means God made something that is not good.

Throughout history, public nakedness went hand in hand with ancient pagan religion. Fashion expert Alison Lurie notes, "...shame seems to have played very little part in development of costume. In ancient Egypt, Crete, and Greece, the naked body was not considered immodest; slaves and athletes habitually went without clothing, while people of high rank wore garments that were cut and draped so as to show a good deal when in motion."

So while a naked body was common for pagans, being without one's outer garment was considered immodest and even shameful among God's people. In fact, at the time of Jesus (peace be upon him), it is this very covering that differentiated the Jewish Romans (monotheists) from the Hellenistic Romans (pagans). Islam, being the Final Revelation of God to humanity, upholds the Abrahamic focus on modesty and humility.

May peace be with you,
Ahmed

CONVERSATION WITH JESSICA – PART 3

Understanding Islamic Law

Email #01 – From: Jessica
Sent: Saturday, July 31, 2010 10:19 a.m.
To: Ahmed Rashed

Is this a good example of your peaceful, loving, and tolerant religion? Or is this just another example of bad Muslims? If good Muslims exist, tell me what country are they in? Are they in Europe, the US, or Canada?

http://edition.cnn.com/2010/WORLD/meast/07/30/iran.stoning/

Email #02 – From: Ahmed Rashed
Sent: Sunday, August 8, 2010 11:01 a.m.
To: Jessica

In the Name of God, the Most-Gracious, the Ever-Merciful:
Dear Jessica,

I apologize for taking so long to respond to this email. My wife was sick with a fever most of last week. Let's proceed with your question:

First of all, we acknowledge the fact that Islam is the fastest growing religion in the world, despite all the negative media attention it is receiving. From this, we conclude there is something behind the headlines that is attracting these men and women to embrace Islam and choose to live by its ethical code.

Secondly, we acknowledge that the popular demand in many Muslim-majority countries for the implementation of Sharia (Islamic law) is seen as a 'threat' to secularism. For this reason, it has aroused suspicion, anger, and hatred among the Western ruling elite who want to dissuade people from sympathizing with Islam. It is for this reason you and I see so many news stories whose only purpose is to vilify anything connected with Islam and especially Islamic law. You must understand this backdrop, Jessica, if you want to understand the larger context of this article and others like it.

Now we will ask four different questions; their purpose is to stimulate thought that will shed light on this issue, God-willing.

1. What is the purpose of Divine Law?
2. What is the role of punishment in Islamic Law?
3. What are the conditions that must be met in order for the moral law to be enforced?
4. Are these conditions being met in the case you cited?

What is the purpose of Divine Law?

Imam Ghazali (a prominent Islamic scholar of the 11th century) wrote: *"The key principle of Islamic Law is preventing harm to people and bringing welfare to them."* This is the basic assumption of the observant Muslim when he encounters a prohibition in the Qur'an or the teachings of the Prophet. A Muslim believes this comprehensive code of behavior (public and private) is the guide by which he can attain God-consciousness and piety, and it is by adhering to this Path that spiritual purification can be achieved at the individual level, the family level, and the community level. God, in His Wisdom, has provided his creation with the perfect blueprint of how to bring about a just and moral society, a society that is God-fearing, pious, and moral.

As we had mentioned before, Islam emphasizes the welfare of the community over the freedom of the individual. So the commandments found in the Qur'an and the teachings of the Prophet are seen as vehicles by which society can be saved from rampant individualism (which is often a sugary word for selfishness), injustice, and immorality. It seeks to enable a society based on justice coupled with mercy to emerge and thrive.

Islamic law recognizes that every human being has the right to life, property, religion, honor, and intellect. Any act by any individual that jeopardizes the life, property, religion, honor, or intellect of another individual is prohibited. Any act by any individual that threatens the life, property, religion, honor, or intellect of a community is not only prohibited, it also is seen as a crime that deserves to be deterred and punished.

What is the role of punishment in Islamic law?

All the above is very nice in theory, you might say, but why is there corporal or capital punishment? Why must people be executed? Where is the mercy in that? The answer is to remember what Uthman ibn Affan (the 3rd Caliph after the Prophet) said about crime and punishment: "The prescribed punishment is to deter those men who are not deterred by fear of God." In other words, the primary purpose of punishment is to deter would-be criminals from committing the crime in the first place. Since "an ounce of prevention is better than a pound of cure," the penal system of Islam seeks to prevent crime in the first place.

The object of punishment is **not** to relentlessly hunt down wrong-doers for retribution, but to see that peace, right, and order are restored. This could be illustrated by the fact that the historical Islamic penal system almost wholly lacks police, prisons, and professional executioners. The prescribed punishments may appear to be harsh, but human experience shows that if a punishment was to act as a deterrent, then it has to be severe and exemplary.

What are the conditions that must be met in order for Islamic law to be enforced?

Let us limit our answer to the aspect of Islamic law that is cited: adultery. In Arabic, the crime and sin of **zina** refers to any act of sexual intercourse (penetration) that occurs outside the bonds of marriage.

Stoning is the most severe of all the punishments that exist in Islamic law. It is extremely rare in practice. During the last fourteen centuries of Islamic history (before the fall of the Islamic Caliphate in 1912), only *"fourteen cases of stoning could be numbered in all that time."* {Iqbal: Islamic Law p.71}

Considering this extreme rarity, it is totally dishonest and unfair for a critic to single out stoning in order to judge not only the Islamic penal system but also the structure of the entire Islamic law in general.

Islamic Law aims to ensure the stability of society from its base — the family — which is the 'nucleus' of society and holds together the various institutions. Chastity is highly esteemed as a supreme virtue in Islamic societies, though it is no longer an ideal in many (but not all) societies in the West.

In the West, the institution of marriage has significantly declined, and nearly half of the marriages end up in divorce. The family has broken down, resulting in the deterioration of society and an increased crime-rate. The root 'cause' of all these is **zina** — the unlawful sexual union between a man and a woman who are not married to each other. *Zina* leads to the breakdown of family ties, depression, domestic violence, child abuse, rape, and sexually transmitted diseases. That's why John Major's "Back to Basics" campaign was geared toward restoration of family values in order to reduce the crime rate and to maintain social order.

Now, to answer the actual question, *what conditions must be met before a judge can pass the sentence of death by stoning*:

1. The culprit must be mature.
2. The culprit must be sane.
3. The culprit must have done the act voluntarily (unforced).
4. The culprit must be in a marriage that has been consummated.
5. The culprit must either be caught in the ACTUAL act of intercourse by four reliable witnesses or give four unforced confessions against themselves on four different occasions. They may retract their confessions at any time.

These are the strict legal technicalities that have to be met before the punishment of stoning is carried out on adulterers. These facts are not highlighted by the West when condemning the punishments for adultery. All the abovementioned conditions have to be met before the punishment is imposed, and this is very hard to do.

As for false witnesses, the Qur'an declares: **As for those who slander chaste women and produce not four reliable witnesses, then stripe them with eighty lashes and never accept their testimony thereafter. (24:4)**

So we see that slander of this kind is dealt with severely, because it seriously affects and damages self-confidence and strains family relations. Islam is never prepared to accept the kind of gossip that is so frequently found in the tabloid papers, and scandal-mongers are punished severely with eighty stripes. If the four witnesses differ in even a minor detail about what they supposedly saw, they are considered slanderers; therefore, the culprit(s) goes free and these witnesses receive eighty lashes. This actually happened at least twice during the reign of Umar (the 2nd Caliph).

That is why during the life of the Prophet, every adultery conviction came about due to confession, not witnessing. Hence, punishment by stoning has remained what it was **meant to be**: harsh in principle, but extremely rare in practice. This punishment may appear severe, but the requirements for conviction are even more severe. The Prophet said: *"Avoid the Divine Punishments as much as possible. Wherever there is even a mild doubt, release him, for releasing by an error on the part of the judge is better than to punish anyone with error."* (recorded by Tirmidi and Ibn Majah)

Are these conditions being met in the case you cited?

The article you cited does not mention the exact details of the case and how the conviction was secured. It is a sin for me to speculate on this woman's status, since I do not have all the information. The Qur'an warns believers not to make judgments until you have all sides of the story and all facts on the table.

If there were actually four witnesses to the woman's adultery, or if she actually gave four unforced confessions, then the sentence is in accordance to the teachings of the Qur'an and the Prophet, and therefore the sentence is just. However, if her confession was forced *(as seems to be mentioned)* or there were not four witnesses to the act, then the sentence does **NOT** meet the requirements of the Qur'an and the Prophet, and therefore the sentence is **NOT** just, and she should be set free.

In conclusion, as many Islamic scholars have pointed out, there are over fifty independent Muslim countries, but *"no country*

What Would a Muslim Say?

is governed exclusively by Islamic law" [Walker p. 651]. Hence "we do not have in the world an Islamic penal system which would be accepted as genuine. Rather we have attempts to recreate the Islamic penal system." [Haroon p.11].

Saudi Arabia alone appears to be the best living example of the application of Islamic law in the modem world, though "the 'spirit' of the Sharia has long since disappeared and the whole of Sharia too is not being enforced." [Mawdudi: Islamic Law p.4].

May peace be with you,
Ahmed Rashed

Email #03 – From: Jessica
Sent: Monday, August 9, 2010 12:42 a.m.
To: Ahmed Rashed

No problem with the delay in your response; we have been on holiday. I hope your wife is feeling better.

Thank you; this is of course insightful, but in our bible it states "Vengeance is mine, saith the Lord." I could not imagine imposing a death sentence on anyone, and my Lord and Savior would never ask this of me. What we Western societies fear from your Islamic faith is this law (Sharia). It is why you are not persecuted in our culture, although we would be in your culture. "Live and let live," seems to be our motto, and perhaps we are afraid this will be taken advantage of. It is true that in numbers you may surpass us, even in the Western cultures. We are fearful of being thrust back two millennia. We are always progressive. My ancestors who left Europe 400-500 years ago were very brave explorers who sought a new land and made a culture where freedom was placed above all. Again, I state we believe in human choice as long as no one is harmed. The Islamic law seems to state that any choice that may offend a prophet is just cause to end a life; four witnesses or no. We have a society of "live and let live." The only equivalent I can see to what you say of Islamic law in Western culture was Nazi Germany.

Although I have been blessed with two sons and no

daughters, I would want for them the same rights and the same freedoms as my sons. It is the way of my ancestors that I always had a choice as a woman. In the case of this particular woman, she was a young woman with young children who was seen in public with a male who was not a relative. Tell me, can any decent person with any discretion really have four witnesses to adultery? Clearly that would rarely happen, even in our own society. Perhaps her motives were innocent. I have spent time with males who were not related to me, and I can assure you there was nothing immodest afoot. I was taught by Catholic nuns for thirteen years, and I appreciate modesty. I do not have impure thoughts for males who may not be related to me. I look at my sons, and I know they will treat women with the same respect that I have been afforded by men that were my husband, my father, my brothers, and even men who were not related to me.

I realize I should have my own King James Version of the bible so I could so eloquently quote the passages of respect, innocence, and caring for your fellow man or woman.

Email #04 – From: Ahmed Rashed
Sent: Monday, August 9, 2010 8:50 p.m.
To: Jessica

In the Name of God, the Most-Gracious, the Ever-Merciful:
Dear Jessica,

Did you actually read my entire email? I ask you this question because, to be honest with you, I felt confused and hurt by your response. Every single point you wrote was *already* addressed in my email.

Email #05 – From: Jessica
Sent: Tuesday, August 10, 2010 12:03 a.m.
To: Ahmed Rashed

I am sorry you feel that way. I did read your message in its entirety; I guess I was a little thrown off by the following statement:

If there were actually four witnesses to the woman's adultery, or if she actually gave four unforced confessions, then the sentence is in accordance to the teachings of the Qur'an and the Prophet, and therefore the sentence is just.

I do not see justice in removing a widowed woman from her young children, imprisoning her for much of their very young lives, and then sentencing her to public humiliation and torture.

Email #06 – From: Ahmed Rashed
Sent: Thursday, August 12, 2010 9:16 a.m.
To: Jessica

Dear Jessica,

It is precisely BECAUSE of the evidence required that I am inclined to believe that this Iranian woman should **not** be stoned. If you read the sentence after the one you quoted me with, you will note that I mentioned the fact that her confession seemed to be forced and that there does not seem to be any witnesses to the actual act.

Jessica, think about it: what is the *significance* of the requirement of four witnesses? It means that this punishment was never MEANT to be implemented on any except the most depraved, shameless, and corrupting individuals.

Let me tell you a true story:

In the 6th year of Hijra, the Prophet was returning home from a battle. During one of their rest stops, his wife, Aisha, got separated from the army when she went to answer the call of nature. When she came back and found that she had been left behind, she sat in the now-empty camp and waited for someone to notice her absence and go back to look for her.

It happened that one of the rear-guard scouts came upon her first. He found Aisha and dismounted, offering her his horse to ride. She sat on the horse, and he walked, leading the animal back to Medina. When the people saw the two enter the city together, some of the less-virtuous Muslims started wagging their tongues about the incident, implying that some infidelity had occurred. Aisha was a young beauty, and the man who found her was also young and handsome. Even with the Prophet and other Companions defending her honor, the gossip that spread for the next few weeks nearly tore the Muslim community apart.

Then God revealed the following verses to vindicate Aisha and admonish the Muslim community: **Those who perpetrated the slander are a group amongst you. Do not consider it bad for you, but it is good for you. Each person among them bears his share in the sin. As for him who played the major role — for him is a terrible punishment. Why, when you heard about it, the believing men and women did not think well of one another, and say, "This is an obvious lie." Why did they not bring four witnesses to testify to it? If they fail to bring the witnesses, then in God's sight, they are liars. (24:11-13)**

See that? In God's eyes, anyone who accuses a woman of adultery and does not bring four witnesses is a **LIAR**. That person is considered a spreader of slander, and his punishment is eighty lashes and his testimony will never be accepted again. This is huge. This shows the intent of mercy behind this seemingly harsh penalty. Seeing a man and woman together is NOT enough to bring the charge of adultery. In fact, such suspicion or speculation is a SIN and a CRIME in Islam.

Not only that, but it is related that there was a prostitute in Medina during the time of the Prophet. It was common knowledge who she was and what she did. However, this woman and her clients were never punished. Why? It is because her immoral activities were never done in such a way to violate the public morality. No one leveled a charge against her for fear of being accused of slandering. So we see that even a woman like this is safe so long as she does not descend into open lewdness and brazen shamelessness. Her case is between herself and God.

Not only that, but during the reign of Umar ibn Al-Khattab (the 2nd Caliph), he was making his rounds around the city when he stumbled upon a couple having sex in a back alley. He recognized them and knew that they were not married to each other. He rushed back to the mosque to inform the other

Companions of what he saw. Ali ibn Abi Talib, a cousin of the Prophet and the chief justice during Umar's rule, rebuked him sharply. He told him, "You do not have any witnesses except yourself." Umar insisted that he saw what he saw and that punishment should be given out. Ali told him flatly, "Bring four witnesses. If you do not have them, and you do not stop this talk, we will charge you with slander and have you lashed." Umar calmed down and realized his error and withdrew his charge. So we see that even the chief of state could not "ignore" the Divine Commandment of four witnesses.

This is the example of good Muslims who understand their faith and know how to live it with justice *and* mercy. **Jessica, this is the level of evidence that the righteous Muslim is supposed to demand before any sentence can be passed.** In fact, Ali (the Justice mentioned above) and ibn Abbas (a Companion of the Prophet who was renowned for his Qur'an knowledge) are famous for saying, "If there is any 'if' or 'maybe' in the case of Islamic law, then the penalty cannot be applied."

Now, the next question you asked was how can such a punishment be justified, even if there are four witnesses?

For this we have to remember that the integrity of the family and the welfare of the society are the two most important values in Islam. These values are more important than any individual right. It is from this concern that we can understand Islamic law. It is true that 'vengeance' belongs only to God, because only He knows all the facts and the proper punishment for any given sin. However, God, in His Wisdom, has also provided guidance and laws for humans to uphold in their societies so as to bring about the best in humanity and to curb what is worst in humanity.

Every human being has the right to CHOOSE to sin or not to sin. Sinners who do not repent will be punished by God in the hereafter, but a sin doesn't become a CRIME unless that *choice* to sin affects families and communities. The purpose of punishment is not to 'play God.' Rather, the purpose is to protect individuals from other individuals who choose to violate their rights or endanger the community. Should not God give his Divine Advice to His people on how to eliminate crime and vice from their community?

Jessica, think about the kind of upbringing children who have adulterous parents have. Think of what the next generation is like if they see their parents being unfaithful. Think, moreover, on the effect of marriage as an institution. The stability of the family is jeopardized by husband or wife giving in to temptations.

Doing such a sin once or twice when no one knows about it is a private affair between that sinner and God. However, if such behavior **persists**, or becomes *commonplace*, or becomes *publicly accepted,* can you honestly say this is a good outcome? Is individual 'freedom' so precious that it is above the welfare and children and future of a society?

A person who knows the harsh punishment for this act gets two messages: first, he knows that what he is about to do is a big deal, not just some little thing. Second, he will think twice before doing it. The harsh punishment is there for the purpose of deterrence, because it would be better to prevent the crime in the first place. Again, I apologize for the long email, and I look forward to your reply.

May peace be with you,
Ahmed

Email #07 – From: Jessica
Sent: Thursday, August 12, 2010 7:36 p.m.
To: Ahmed Rashed

I understand everything you say. I like your story. In my culture we call it morality. It is something that exists in each of us in our higher self. Even if someone gets away with it, our higher self always knows what is right and what is wrong. Even for innocent children raised with immorality, they know what is right and wrong like second nature.

For example, I got married at age twenty. I have just had my 25th wedding anniversary. I am very fortunate that my husband is both a good husband and a good father. Once I had children, my life was no longer my life, and every decision I made was based on their protection and well-being. It is perhaps because my husband's parents never divorced and neither did mine, and hopefully my children will also marry happily "by choice" and be good husbands, fathers, and citizens of society.

I could not help but notice today that they have after all this long time upgraded the charges against this woman from adultery to murder of her husband to justify the death penalty. This does sadden me. It saddens me that her children who had already lost their father then lost their mother to prison when they were very young. I think it is harder for me to accept the fate of her children than her punishment, and I am sure it is the same for her.

Meanwhile, if my twenty-year-old son is dating a Muslim woman, and he is not of her culture. Should I be concerned for him and also for her? Would she be afforded the same choice my son has? I realize that a mixed marriage, even if it is of different Christians such as Protestant and Catholic, can be difficult, not to mention Jewish and Catholic relationships. I think it is very sad that there is one God and yet there is such division. I often think should the Christian faiths unite as the Muslims do that they would be a much stronger representation, but alas, there are many divisions within our own Christian faith. Do Muslims have the same division if they are Saudi Muslim or if they are Afghan or Iranian Muslim? It does not appear to me that they do.

I like to read, so I do not at all mind a long response.

God be with you.

Email #08 – From: Ahmed Rashed
Sent: Sunday, August 15, 2010 12:23 p.m.
To: Jessica

Dear Jessica,

Sorry for taking so long to get back to you. Ramadan started Wednesday, so we've been very busy.

To proceed:

Morality is one of the most precious things parents can teach their children. If a child is raised with a strong and correct sense of morality, it means they are ready to take their place in the world without need of constant supervision. If you teach children to do the right thing because you are watching over them, then when you are not watching them, they will do wrong. But if you teach children to do the right thing because God is watching over them, then they are less likely to do wrong, even if you are not around.

As for the Iranian woman, there are two more points I would like to make.

The first is that since we don't know all the facts, it is not appropriate to judge the verdict. There is a story in the Qur'an about Prophet David (peace be upon him) where two men came to him with a dispute for him to arbitrate. He listened to the plaintiff and then passed judgment, and then God revealed to him that he had done injustice because he passed judgment after hearing only one side of the story. From this Muslims learn that even if a case touches our hearts, we must have all information from both sides before deciding who is right or wrong. For this reason, you see me hesitant to make any decisive statement about the case.

The second is that if all information really was known, we may agree with the verdict. I was reading some blogs about her, and there was one Iranian comment that caught my eye.

Basically the guy was saying that not everything is being told in the Western media, so a lot of the outrage is based on ignorance of the details in the case. He said that not only did she cheat on her husband, she helped her lover murder, cut up, and bury her husband. His point was do you really think such a woman would be a good and safe mother for the children of the man she helped murder? Now, I don't know if his comment is true or not, but since I'm not there, I am really not in a place to say anything, am I?

My point is that it is not fair for anyone to judge the case without knowing all the facts. It is like the O.J. Simpson trial

What Would a Muslim Say?

several years ago; everyone had an opinion, but the only ones who have the right to make a judgment were the judge and jury in the case who got all the information. So they came to a conclusion based on their information and not based on the news stories.

As for your son dating a Muslim woman, I don't understand why this would worry you. I also don't understand what you meant by "Would she be afforded the same choice my son has?" Perhaps if you explain this concern in a different way, I could better respond.

As for difference between different groups of Muslims, the differences do exist, but they are much smaller than the differences between Jewish groups and between Christian groups. Most non-Muslims would not notice the difference. That is because the definition of Islam was clearly taught by many verses of Qur'an and many sayings of the Prophet.

I look forward to your reply.

May peace be with you,

Ahmed

With Dialogue Comes Understanding

CONVERSATION WITH MARLENE

Etiquettes of Visiting a Mosque

Email #02 – From: Marlene
Sent: Tuesday, January 25, 2011 12:43 a.m.
To: Ahmed Rashed

Mr. Rashed

First of all I would like to thank you for the thorough introduction. I have been looking for a mosque so I can check out the Friday service, but I have some questions to ask and hope that they are not too silly.

1. Are all services in Arabic?
2. I have heard that there is a separate entrance for women and they stay in the back, is this true?
3. Other than covering my hair, what are the other rules about dressing (like in some faiths women have to wear dresses that are to at least mid-calf).
4. After the service, can I go to the pastor and ask questions? I know that is not the right title, but it is the one I know.
5. Is there a certain lady I can talk to about women and Islam?

Like I said, I hope it is no too silly, but I do want to go to a service and do not want to offend anyone, even though I have never been in a mosque. And if there is any information you can give me, that would be great.

Thank Yyou
Marlene

Email #03 – From: Ahmed Rashed
Sent: Wednesday, January 26, 2011 11:33 a.m.
To: Marlene

Ms. Marlene:

You are very welcome. Our purpose is to serve and educate; there are no silly questions. :)

1. No. The ritual prayer itself is always recited in Arabic, but during the "quite periods" every congregant whispers his/her own supplication in whichever language he/she wishes.

What Would a Muslim Say?

The Friday sermon usually has an Arabic introduction and conclusion, but most mosques have the main body of the sermon in English. In mosques with mostly immigrant congregations, the first half of the sermon is given in Arabic/Turkish/Urdu while the second half is the translation in English.

2. This is true for some mosques, but not for all. Each mosque has its own "culture" regarding male/female separation. It **is** true that the Prophet instructed his followers that women should not pray in the same lines as men, so all mosques observe separation during the formal ritual prayer.

However, in some mosques this means they have a separate room, in other mosques they line up behind the men, and in some mosques women and men pray in the same hall but with the women on the right and the men on the right with a divider or curtain separating them. You can contact the mosque you plan on visiting and ask them about these logistics.

As for entrances, some mosques have one large entrance that everyone uses, and some have separate entrances. Again, you can call ahead to find out what is normal. If you go to www.IslamicFinder.org and type in your city or zip, you can find listings of local mosques with their phone numbers and addresses.

3. Here is the dress code for my local mosque. We made it general because we get people from many different backgrounds. It should be sufficient for your visit:

Dress Code: We require all visitors to wear appropriate dress while in the mosque. We ask that group leaders ensure their students maintain a proper standard of dress, which displays respect for mosque etiquettes.

- Shorts are not allowed for either gender. Pants or skirts should be <u>loose</u> and <u>ankle-length</u>.
- T-shirts with inappropriate or explicit pictures/phrases are not allowed for either gender.
- Women are requested to wear long-sleeve shirts and headscarves that cover <u>hair</u> and <u>neck</u>.

4. The name for the leader of the mosque is imam (pronounced EE-maam). The best way is to call ahead and make an appointment; that way, the imam will go to his office after the service and see you there. If that doesn't work (most mosques do not have any secretaries to answer phone calls), you could simply go to the mosque and ask any congregant (man or woman), "Excuse me, I would like to talk to the imam, please." Anyone who gets this request will usually rush to him and let him know before he leaves that there is a visitor that wants to speak to him. Mosques are very informal, so this is not seen as impolite or anything.

5. There is no specific position for women's affairs, if that's what you mean. Usually, there are volunteers and sometimes a secretary, but it all depends on the mosque. Call the mosque and ask if there is a woman who is active in the community you can talk to. If you are lucky enough to find a secretary, she can probably be your first contact. If not, again, mosques are very informal, so just ask any congregant you find and let them know that you want to talk to someone about women and Islam.

The best information I can give you is the IslamicFinder.org website. It has some articles, but the best thing about it is that it lists all Islamic centers, schools, and businesses in the area you search.

I hope this addressed your concerns. Feel free to email me if you have any other questions or topics you want to discuss.

May peace be with you,

Ahmed

CONVERSATION WITH WINSTON

God's Grace and Free Will

Email #02 – From: Winston
Sent: Wednesday, February 22, 2011 5:15 p.m.
To: Ahmed Rashed

Two questions about verses in the Qur'an: 1) V2:6 and V2:7 (i.e., in the second Surah on verse six and seven) appears to mean that the reason people disbelieve in Islam is because Allah desires it, but if that is true then people do not have any free will to accept or reject Islam. Do human beings have complete free will, or is it limited or is there none? 2) Regarding V2:24, does this statement mean that anyone who is not a Muslim will be punished by Allah? If this is true, then are non-Muslims who have good thoughts and performing good deeds also going to be punished after death? In other words, is it possible to be a good person and not be a Muslim?

Email #03 – From: Ahmed Rashed
Sent: Wednesday, February 23, 2011 6:26 a.m.
To: Winston

In the Name of God, the Most-Gracious, the Ever-Merciful:
Your first question regarding (2:6-7) refers to the leaders of Quraysh who had heard the Prophet's preaching for over thirteen years and still refused to accept that he was truly sent by God. In addition to refusing belief, they used their power and influence to prevent others from believing in the Prophet. This prevention took the form of persecution, verbal and physical abuse, economic boycott, and beatings, torture and killing. These opening verses were revealed in the first few years after the Prophet migrated from Mecca to Medina (14-15 years after first receiving revelation), and their purpose was to console the Prophet, for he was eager for all the people to believe and follow the guidance he was sent with. God informed him that none would believe except those who received God's grace. And God's grace is not granted unless the person himself turns his heart towards God.

The Qur'an teaches that God guides those who *want* to be guided and leaves astray those who *do not wish to receive guidance*, like the leaders of Quraysh referred to in (2:6-7).

We read this in the Qur'an: **Then when they turned away, God turned their hearts away. (61:5)**

But because they broke their covenant, We cursed them, and made their hearts grow hard. (5:13)

God's granting or withholding His grace is a result of the heart **choosing** to turn towards Him or away from Him. If the choices we made were *not* genuine, it would be **injustice** for God to hold us accountable for them. Since God is *The Just, The Forbearing,* and *The Truth,* we understand that our choices are real. The Qur'an affirms this by ending many different verses with the following phrase: **This is for what you yourself have done, and never is God unjust to His creatures.**

As for your second question, the verse (2:23-24) is simply a challenge to those who doubt that the Qur'an is really from God. It says to compose a chapter as eloquent and profound. Since the Arabs were at the peak of their literary abilities at that time, and since Muhammad was a simple, illiterate man never known for any poetic ability in the forty years of life before revelation, the challenge is a strong one even in this day and age.

As for your question about what happens to non-Muslims, the Qur'an says: **And whoever seeks a religion other than Islam, it will not be accepted from him, and he will be one of the losers in the Hereafter. (3:85)**

This may seem extreme, but as mentioned in the first email, it is written in the Qur'an that God sent prophets to each nation in history. In other words, God made a covenant with every people in every time. This covenant was "*Islam*," which means surrender and obedience to God, and a person who surrenders his will to God and obeys His commandments is called a "*Muslim*." The primary condition for salvation is faith in God and directing all worship exclusively to God.

This understanding is confirmed by the Qur'an: **The believers, the Jews, the Christians, and the Sabaeans — all who believed in God and the Last Day and do good deeds — will be rewarded by their Lord; they shall have no fear, nor shall they grieve. (2:62)**

This means that those from the previous nations, who faithfully followed the AUTHENTIC teachings of their Prophets (Jesus, Moses, Abraham, etc.), will receive God's mercy and forgiveness.

As for those who never met a prophet, let me show you a quote from Dr. Sherman Jackson, a well-known Muslim scholar at the University of California. He translated many classical books and is well respected in the field. In his introduction to Imam al-Ghazali's famous book, *Theological Tolerance*, Dr. Jackson explains this issue as follows:

Al-Ghazali goes on, however, to insist that God's mercy will encompass non-Muslims as well, including "most of the Christians of Byzantium and the [non-Muslim] Turks of the age." These people he divides into three categories: 1) those who never heard so much as the name Muhammad; 2) those who heard his name and had access to concrete and authentic information about his life and mission; 3) those who heard of him but received wrong, insufficient, or misleading information about this life and mission. According to al-Ghazali, it is only those of the second category, who came into reliable and concrete information about Muhammad and, in a spirit of defiance, persist in rejecting his prophethood, who will dwell forever in Hellfire. This is because only such people can be said to be guilty of deeming the Prophet to be a liar. As for those of the first and third categories, these will be covered by God's all-encompassing mercy. For, ultimately, their non-acceptance of Muhammad's prophethood is free of defiance and attributable to circumstances beyond their control.

Let me know if you would like more in-depth information or if you have any follow-up questions. I look forward to your response, Winston, and I hope to continue the discussion.

May peace be with you,

Ahmed Rashed

What Would a Muslim Say?

Email #04 – From: Winston
Sent: Friday, February 25, 2011 11:43 a.m.
To: Ahmed Rashed

Hello,

Thank you for taking time from your busy schedule to respond to my email. Could you please help me understand these two verses from the Qur'an? (1) Regarding V2:34, do angels have free will? If angels do not have free will, then how can Iblis choose to reject Allah? If angels are free to reject or accept Islam, then what happens to all the angels who rejected it? (2) Regarding V2:61, who were the Sabians? Do the Sabians still exist now?

Always grateful,
Winston

Email #05 – From: Ahmed Rashed
Sent: Friday, February 25, 2011 3:42 p.m.
To: Winston

In the Name of God, the Most-Gracious, the Ever-Merciful:

No problem, Winston; I am glad to be of service. To proceed with your questions:

The angels are intelligent beings that God created from light. They are luminous creatures with no physical bodies. They do not eat, drink, or procreate; they are above animal desires, sins, and mistakes. They do not have human characteristics, but they can, with God's permission, appear in the form of human beings. They are not gods, nor are they the sons or daughters of God. The relationship of the angels to God is that of absolute service, obedience, and submission to His commands. They do not have free will and are in constant submission to God, carrying out His work and executing His commands as He pleases.

So If Angels cannot disobey God, what about Satan?

Satan — whose name in Arabic is "Iblis" — questioned God's appointment of fallible humans to the honorable position of stewardship. Iblis disobeyed God and refused to prostrate himself to Adam. The Qur'an says: **When We said to the angels,**

'Prostrate yourselves before Adam,' all prostrated themselves except Satan. He was one of the Jinn and he disobeyed his Lord's command. Do you then take him and his offspring as protectors instead of Me, despite their enmity? What an evil exchange for the wrongdoers! (18:50)

This is one difference between the Biblical and Qur'anic narrative. Iblis is not an angel or a fallen angel. Angels cannot disobey God, so angels cannot fall. Satan was from the Jinn, described in the Qur'an in this passage: **We created man out of dry clay, from molded mud, and the Jinn We had created before from flaming fire. (15:26-27)**

So the Jinn are a creation that is part of the Unseen World like angels, but they are able to choose between obedience and disobedience, like men. There are good, believing Jinn and evil, wicked Jinn. To understand the relationship between Jinn and Men, we continue reading this passage from the Qur'an: **Your Lord said to the angels, "I am about to bring into being a man wrought from mud. When I have formed him and breathed My spirit into him, fall down in prostration before him," then the angels all prostrated themselves together. But Satan did not; he refused to join those who prostrated themselves.**

God asked him, "What is the matter with you that you are not among those who have prostrated themselves?" He replied, "I am not one to prostrate myself to a man whom You have created out of clay of molded mud."

God said, "Then get out of here; for you are accursed, and the curse shall be on you till the Day of Judgment!" Satan said, "O my Lord! Grant me respite till the Day of Resurrection." He said, "You are granted respite till that Appointed Day." He said, "My Lord, since You have let me go astray, I shall beautify for them the path of evil on earth and I shall mislead them all, except for Your chosen servants."

God said, "This is the path which leads straight to Me. Surely, you shall have no power over My true servants, except the misguided who choose to follow you. Surely, Hell is the place to which they are destined." (15:28-43)

What Would a Muslim Say?

So the first source of evil is Satan and all the evil, wicked Jinn that follow him; they spend their days and nights whispering suggestions into the hearts of Adam's progeny. The other source of evil is the selfish inclination of the soul of the person itself. The satanic forces are defeated by constant remembrance, repentance, and prayer. The selfish forces are defeated by worship, discipline, obeying God's commands, and living the Prophetic lifestyle.

As for the Sabians in the other verse, there are two interpretations that the classical commentators mention. The first one (slight majority) is that they are a subgroup of People of the Book — not Jews, not Christians, and not around anymore. The second one (slight minority) is that they are any people who reject the established organized religions of their society and turn to direct worship of God without any Prophet or Scripture to follow. This second opinion includes people who lived after the time of Prophet Muhammad but never heard of his message or the Qur'an or met any Muslims.

May peace be with you,
Ahmed

Email #06 – From: Winston
Sent: Friday, March 4, 2011 8:03 a.m.
To: Ahmed Rashed

Hello Ahmed,

Thank you for responding to my previous questions. Could you please help to understand the following verses from the Qur'an? (1) Regarding V2:74, what is the meaning of this metaphor? (2) Regarding V2:88, what exactly is the curse Allah has placed on the Jewish people? If Allah has placed a curse on all Jewish people, then that means the unborn children of future generations will get the curse. However, according to V2:286 (if I read it correctly) each person is responsible for their own sins.

How can one group of people be cured throughout time for the sins made by those in the distant past? V2:286 is the following:

"God does not burden a soul beyond capacity. Each will enjoy what (good) he earns, as indeed each will suffer from (the wrong) he does. Punish us not, O Lord, if we fail to remember or lapse into error. Burden us not, O Lord, with a burden as You did those before us. Impose not upon us a burden, O Lord, we cannot carry. Overlook our trespasses and forgive us, and have mercy upon us; You are our Lord and Master, help us against the clan of unbelievers."

The translation is from *Al-Qur'an* by Ahmed Ali.

Always grateful,

Winston

**Email #07 – From: Ahmed Rashed
Sent: Tuesday, March 8, 2011 10:42 a.m.
To: Winston**

In the Name of God, the Most-Gracious, the Ever-Merciful:

Hello Winston,

So, regarding 2:74, this verse is saying that the hearts of these people became not just "as hard as a rock" but rather became "harder than rock." For it is an observable fact that some rocks are split by rivers that run through them (canyons and waterfalls come to mind), and other rocks are split by even smaller amounts of water (think of mudslides or streams that happen just after a rain), and other rocks crack/split on their own. So each metaphor shows a rock splitting due to weaker and weaker impact (river, rain, on their own), and therefore the comparison is that the hearts of these men who witnessed a miracle of resurrection and still were obstinate are even harder than rocks.

As for 2:88, this is referring to the immediate community of those who denied and/or killed prophets before and were threatening to do the same to Prophet Muhammad. Every human being, regardless of his upbringing or parents' religion, has a chance to learn the truth and accept it. However, the curse does not fall except on those who received Signs and Prophets and still refuse to accept. Notice that v2:87 talks about those who denied

Moses and Jesus, whereas v2:88-89 talk about those who denied Muhammad. This means those who WITNESSED and MET these great Prophets and still chose not to follow them for some contrived reason. This is indicated by the end of 2:87: **Is it ever so, that, when there cometh unto you a Messenger with that which ye yourselves desire not, ye grow arrogant and some ye disbelieve and some ye slay?**

May peace be with you,
Ahmed

Email #08 – From: Winston
Sent: Wednesday, March 9, 2011 9:08 a.m.
To: Ahmed Rashed

Hello Ahmed,

Thank you for responding to my previous questions. However, you did not completely answer my second question. Verse 2:88 in the Qur'an mentions a curse. The verse seems to imply that the curse is that *a person will not believe in Islam completely or at all.* But this is really the cause, not the effect of the curse. Otherwise, if the **act of disbelieving** is itself a curse of Allah, then it is not the people who are choosing to accept or reject Islam. Since people have free will, that is they can make decisions without Allah interfering, then the curse must be something else. Can you define, in detail, what the curse is?

Always grateful,
Winston

Email #09 – From: Ahmed Rashed
Sent: Monday, March 14, 2011 12:27 p.m.
To: Winston

In the Name of God, the Most-Gracious, the Ever-Merciful:

Hello Winston,

First of all, I apologize for the delay in responding. Let us start with an excerpt from our Islam101 lecture about Divine Decree, Destiny, and Grace:

Islam teaches that God, *The Giver*, has honored humanity with the ability to choose between right and wrong. This gift comes with great responsibility, and we will be accountable for our use of this gift on Judgment Day.

Human free will does not contradict the fact that God, *The Witness*, knows everything that will ever occur in creation. Some might say, "If God knows I am going to commit a sin tomorrow, then it is unavoidable because what God knows will come to pass." Islam teaches that God's knowledge of our decision is a consequence of his being *The All-Knowing*, not a consequence of our being forced to make that decision. His knowledge is perfect and infinite; therefore it is illogical that anything could be hidden from Him or surprising to Him.

Human free will does not contradict the fact that nothing happens in creation except what God wills. Some might say, "Therefore, I have no free will; it is just an illusion." Islam teaches that God created within each of us the **ability** to formulate an intention. God wants us to be able to make our own choices. When a person makes a choice, God, by His divine will, creates the actions and circumstances that allow or disallow the person's intention to be carried out.

God guides those who want to be guided and leaves astray those who do not wish to receive guidance. We read this in the Qur'an: **Then when they turned away, God turned their hearts away (61:5)**

But because they broke their covenant, We cursed them, and made their hearts grow hard. (5:13)

Now let us dig into the translation a little bit. The actual word used in the verse mentioned is **"la-a-na,"** which is usually translated as "he cursed." The opposite word linguistically is **"na-a-ma"** which is usually translated as "he graced." What I am trying to point out is that just as God bestows his Grace on those who seek Him and turn to Him, He also withholds His Grace from those who deny Him or consistently turn away from Him. That is the Islamic understanding of God's "curse."

So those who continue to turn away and disobey and defy God time and time again will eventually seal themselves off from God's Grace. This is supported by many sayings of the Prophet, many verses in the Qur'an, and many sayings of the scholars as well. God's Grace and mercy is open to any and all who come to Him with sincerity and humility. But those who do not come to him, or do so with arrogance or some sense of entitlement, will not receive God's Grace.

More importantly for our discussion, when a human being exercises his free will time and time again to turn away from God's Grace, then **and only then** does God decree this person to be beyond redemption. In other words, God has sealed his fate. However, this decree of God is not arbitrary, nor is it tyrannical, for it is the many actions of the free agent human being himself that have sealed his own fate. It is the accumulation of unrepented sins that result in that person being cut off from God's Grace.

This concept is similar to the Old Testament description of Pharaoh in the story of Moses. It is said of Pharaoh that "his heart was hardened." Again, who hardened his heart? Obviously, God (who has power over all things) is the one who hardened his heart. But what is the cause of this hardening? It is nothing more than the defiance and arrogance of Pharaoh himself.

God never withholds His Grace the first time a person sins or defies Him, nor the second, nor the tenth, nor even the hundredth. It is when sinning and defiance and arrogance become that person's way of life of that God makes his Decree.

It is this kind of people that the verse is referencing. Feel free to contact me with more questions along this line, or if you have other topics you would like to discuss.

May peace be with you,

Ahmed

Email #10 – From: Winston
Sent: Tuesday, March 15, 2011 9:22 p.m.
To: Ahmed Rashed

Hello Ahmed,

Thank you. Your response to my last question was very enlightening. You do not need to apologize for any delay. I appreciate any effort you can make to answer my questions. Can you please help me to understand the following verses?

(1) Regarding verse 2:275, is the act of earning interest forbidden by Allah? If this is true, then having a savings account with a bank, owning stocks on Wall Street, a career in the financial industry, etc. is also forbidden.

(2) Regarding verse 3:39, this verse seems to state that the prophet 'Isa (peace be upon him) will practice celibacy. Is there any passage in the Qur'an which mentions that 'Isa (peace be upon him) was married? There are none in the third sura. From what I understand of Islam, each prophet of Allah (peace be upon them) is a role model of a Muslim, and all Muslims must emulate them as much as possible. If it is true that 'Isa (peace be upon him) had intentionally chosen not to get married, then all Muslims must practice celibacy.

Always grateful,
Winston

Email #11 – From: Ahmed Rashed
Sent: Friday, March 18, 2011 11:31 a.m.
To: Winston

In the Name of God, the Most-Gracious, the Ever-Merciful:

Hello Winston,

It seems you are reading through the Qur'an and asking questions along the way. Is this so, or are you doing focused study?

(1) Interest is forbidden, whether giving or taking. So yes, all the things you list are also forbidden. The Prophet also predicted that there would come a day when nobody would be

safe from his/her wealth being tainted by interest in some way or form. Most scholars believe this prediction to be actualized in this day of interest-based financing and debt-based economy.

One small clarification — there is nothing intrinsically forbidden about owning stock in a company and trading these stocks/shares on the open market. What makes it forbidden is the fact that every business in the market puts its money in interest-bearing accounts for savings, investments, and so on. So any return on investment, profit-sharing, or capital gains are tainted with interest that gets passed on the shareholder.

(2) No. First of all, this verse refers to the son of Zachariah, not Jesus. In the Qur'an, the son of Zachariah is called Yahya; in the Bible, he is called John the Baptist.

The Prophet predicted that when Jesus returns to earth, he will come as a ruler. He will establish justice, marry, have children, and then die a natural death. There is no contradiction between Yahya being unmarried and Muslims being encouraged to marry. Why? For one thing, Yahya never commanded people to abstain from marriage. For another thing, the final messenger's teachings supersede any previous prophet's teachings.

It has always been the case that a prophet would inform his followers which of his practices are mandatory to emulate and which are praiseworthy but only binding on himself. For example, the Prophet Muhammad always prayed long hours before dawn. This prayer is praiseworthy for Muslims to do, but it was not mandatory. Also, the wives of the Prophet were required to cover their faces (the **niqab** or face-veil). This is a virtuous act for other Muslim women to do, but it is not mandatory.

May peace be with you,
Ahmed

With Dialogue Comes Understanding

What Would a Muslim Say?

CONVERSATION WITH LILIAN

Are Islamic Rulings Static or Dynamic?

Email #02 – From: Lilian
Sent: Thursday, February 23, 2011 8:40 p.m.
To: Ahmed Rashed

Question about Islam — what are the authoritative sources of knowledge in Islam? What is the path between Allah and my own consciousness? If I understand correctly, the hierarchy is Word of Allah (the Qur'an), then the Hadith (the sayings of the Prophet), then consensus among scholars, and finally there's me, able to make my own decisions based on my perceptions of what is necessary for a good life. At what point can an individual make their own decision, using intelligent skepticism to examine a situation? At what point does it stop becoming "submission to the will of Allah" and becomes "an individual cherry-picking what makes sense to them?" How can both of those coexist, and who is the authority to judge where the line is crossed or not crossed and based on what proof? Thanks!

Email #03 – From: Ahmed Rashed
Sent: Thursday, February 24, 2011 9:51 a.m.
To: Lilian

In the Name of God, the Most-Gracious, the Ever-Merciful:

Your question is basically about the Limits of Ijtihad. Ijtihad is the science of deriving religious rulings via textual analysis, reasoning, induction, and analogy. It would be beneficial to know the context of your circumstances and inquiry.

Have you already accepted Islam? If so, how long ago was this? What brought this question to mind? Are there any specific examples or rulings that you want to examine? These questions are just so we can build the foundation of our conversation, and so we can address the root issue of Ijtihad in a fruitful way.

I look forward to your reply, Lilian.

May peace be with you,

Ahmed Rashed

Email #04 – From: Lilian
Sent: Thursday, February 24, 2011 2:41 p.m.
To: Ahmed Rashed

As-salaamu alaykum Ahmed!

I have not yet become a Muslim. From what I understand of anti-apostasy laws, being a Muslim is a lifelong commitment, so I want to make sure I educate myself well before I officially become a Muslim. In the meantime, I practice five daily prayers, I learn to recite, I read the Qur'an, and I engage in dialogue with Muslims everywhere I can.

Itjtihad is exactly the topic that interests me. It seems that the main schools of jurisprudence closed the doors to Itjtihad a few centuries ago. Is that not somewhat dangerous to lock ourselves in like this with no flexibility to adapt and reinterpret given our ever-changing context and the ever-changing diversity of cultures embracing Islam? The daily realities of an Inuit person in the far Arctic are very different from the conditions and cultural context during which Muhammad (peace be upon him) lived during the time of revelation.

For instance, I grew up as part of the Queer community in the West, specifically in Canada. So I have many values regarding sexual orientation, gender identity, and human rights that seem incompatible with strict adherence to traditional Fiqh. If I understand correctly, premarital and extramarital relationships are not allowed in Islam. Homosexual acts are punishable by death. Masturbation is also not allowed. To my understanding, the only way Islam allows us to contextualize the human sex drive in a healthy space is to get married and sleep with one's spouse. If this is so, this leaves homosexuals many difficult questions. Do I:

- Look at a way for Islam to allow a same-sex marriage or to at least recognize the same-sex marriage I obtained according to my country's laws?
- Consider that homosexuals who want to become Muslims must in effect make a vow of chastity? Stop having sex forever. Consensual sex in the privacy of my home is evil.

- Continue to have long-term relationships with another woman, despite being Muslim and live with the knowledge that I'm doing sinful activity and contextualize our consensual mutual support and love in a framework of guilt and negativity?
- Lie and pretend not to be sexually repulsed by men. Get married and engage in a relationship with a man despite this being hypocritical?
- Take medication such as antidepressants to eliminate my sex drive?
- Find a more realistic branch of Islam, such as Sufism or Ismaili, where homosexuality is not a big taboo. However, if possible, I would prefer to belong to the great community of traditional orthodox Islam, e.g.. the Sunni tradition, and not to a minority subgroup.

From what I understand of the cultures of Muslim-majority countries, the tradition regarding homosexuality is "don't ask, don't tell." But this is clearly not sustainable in the information age. Homosexuality exists and is defined in the human rights laws of my country. It is illegal to harass gays and lesbians and only shows ignorance to deny their existence and their struggles.

Peace,

Lilian

Email #05 – From: Ahmed Rashed
Sent: Sunday, February 27, 2011 9:30 a.m.
To: Lilian

In the Name of God, the Most-Gracious, the Ever-Merciful:

Let us start with the general and work our way to the specific. First of all, the "gates of Ijtihad" have NOT been closed. I do not understand how this misconception is still in circulation. This was a popular theory among the Islamic scholars of the 18th century. However, colonial domination and rapid technological change forced Islamic scholars across the board to revisit many previous rulings to make them relevant to their times. Ijtihad is alive and well in this day and age, even in Saudi Arabia.

So what are the conditions where such Ijtihad would be seen as legitimate and not just cherry-picking and wishful-thinking? Let us look to the Qur'an on the subject: **Surely, for men and women who have surrendered [to God] — believing men and believing women, obedient men and obedient women, truthful men and truthful women, patient men and patient women, humble men and humble women, charitable men and charitable women, fasting men and fasting women, men and women who guard their chastity, men and women who are ever mindful of God — God is ready with forgiveness and an immense reward. It is not fitting for a believing man or woman to exercise any choice in his or her own affairs once God and His Messenger have reached a decision upon them. Anyone who disobeys God and His Messenger is in manifest error. (33:35-36)**

Now let us look at a well-known authentic saying of the Prophet: *The Prophet sent Mu`adh to Yemen and asked him: "How will you judge the cases?" He replied: "I will judge according to the Book of Allah." The Prophet asked: "But if you do not get anything there, what will you do?" He said: "I will refer to the Sunnah of the Prophet." The Prophet asked: "But if you do not get it even there, what will you do?" He replied: "I will exercise my judgment." Hearing this, the Prophet patted Mu`adh on the shoulder and said: "Praise be to Allah who has guided the Messenger of His Messenger to what pleases His Messenger."*

So as you said, we go to the Qur'an first, then the Sunnah (the example of the Prophet), then the understanding of the Companions, and then finally the personal interpretation of a qualified scholar. So what does this entail? There are many classifications of texts that are used to see if a decisive ruling has been stipulated by the Qur'an, the Sunnah, or the Companions. I will mention only the top three:

- Conditional vs. Unconditional
- Specific vs. General
- Implicit vs. Explicit

Without going into too much gory details, **if** the text of the Qur'an, or the Hadith, or the saying of a Companion **can be shown** to be Explicit or General or Unconditional, **then** the ruling of the text is DECISIVE and therefore not open to further interpretation (as per the above verse). Furthermore, **if** the text-in-question is Conditional or Specific, and it **can be shown** that the situation-in-question meets the Conditions or Specification of the text-in-question, **then** again the ruling of the text is DECISIVE and so not open to further interpretation. Only if both of these two if-statements are false can a scholar legitimately make a ruling that is different from previous rulings.

So what is the ruling and proofs for Islam's stance on homosexuality? From the Qur'an, we have the people of Lot: **Do you, of all people, approach males, and leave your wives whom your Lord has created for you? You are a people who transgress all bounds. (26:165-166)**

In Hadith, the Prophet clarifies the gravity of this sin by saying: *"Allah curses the one who does the actions of the people of Lot"* repeating it three times. He also said, *"If a man comes upon a man then they are both adulterers."*

All of these verses and sayings are explicit in their condemnation of sexual relations between men. Also, none of these texts are Conditional on some external circumstance or context. Therefore, it is unanimous from classical and modern scholars that the ruling on homosexuality is not open to further interpretation, because the Qur'an and the Prophet have both made decisive statements against it. It is understood that if man-man relations are transgression, so too are woman-woman relations.

So what is the wisdom or fairness behind such a ruling?

Islam considers homosexual *behavior* to be the result of a choice. Inclinations do exist within humans for a variety of natural and unnatural acts, from fornication to rape and from necrophilia to bestiality. These inclinations may come from evil suggestions, media influence, or even from direct contact and/or environment. Human beings are not robots, only doing what they are programmed to do. Humans choose, and God holds them responsible for their choices. Were homosexuality a product of genetic destiny, it would be unfair for God to criminalize it and punish those who practice it. Currently, some scientists are even claiming that murder is of genetic origin. To accept that would mean to excuse murderers and tolerate murder.

Homosexuality, like most other traits, is caused by a mix of genes and environment, although we don't know how much of each for every case. This is basic genetics. The same goes for alcoholism and other "bad habits."

The Prophet said: "*A man should not see the private parts of another man, and a woman should not see the private parts of another woman, and a man should not lie with another man under one covering, and a woman should not lie with another woman under one covering.*" He also instructed parents to separate their children in their beds by the age of ten. Clearly, these statements seem aimed at preventing incestuous and homosexual experiences. Such experiences may be reinforced by contacts in schools and/or abuse from adults. Thus, from the Islamic perspective, certain principles are applied at a very early age to prevent certain feelings from developing that could lead to un-Islamic behavior. The point of this paragraph is that the existence of homosexual tendencies or inclinations (same-sex attraction) are **not denied** by Islam or the Prophet; rather, these tendencies or inclinations are seen as real but the Prophet taught that *ACTIONS* based on those desires should be avoided.

Homosexual desires and tendencies are viewed as something which can be **overcome** by *controlling* one's self. Just as one might have an inclination towards overeating or excessive heterosexual behavior, one might have an inclination to same-sex attraction. No doubt controlling this inclination is a struggle, but surely this energy can be channeled in healthier directions, such as prayer and meditation, or anything else that promotes goodness.

So what is a homosexual who wants to enter Islam expected do? Well ... there are two kinds of answers to this question, the legal answer and the personal answer.

The legal answer is that a homosexual should stop their sexual relations with the same sex. In addition, as you hinted at in your email, a person's companions influence their viewpoints, so it would be encouraged for a homosexual to distance themselves from that lifestyle and the people who practice and promote that lifestyle. Finally, the homosexual must acknowledge that they are not at all different from those who have been conditioned to fornicate, or commit theft or murder, or who have become addicted to watching pornography or even television, for that matter. All of these are destructive habits that one learns through continuous exposure or conditioning. So they must ask themselves whether they would prefer to continue in this destructive behavior or make a change.

Islam is full of examples of those who were addicted to all sorts of crimes and sins, but eventually they changed their lives around by affirming faith and commitment in Allah and working diligently upon themselves. The Arabs before Islam were addicted to drinking, womanizing, gambling, and all kinds of vices, and yet after having embraced Islam, they became a better breed of people, breaking free of all such vices.

The personal answer to you, Lilian, really depends on your response to this email. I do not know how far you are in your search for Truth. Nor do I know what has brought you this point in your life. Nor do I know what experiences you had in childhood and young adulthood that formed the feelings and beliefs you have now. However, I am open to continuing this conversation, Lilian, and trying to find answers to these questions together, if you are also inclined to do so.

May peace be with you,
Ahmed

Note: After this dialogue, I came across an article on the topic that presents a unique perspective and a further refinement to what I had written. You can find it here:
http://muslimmatters.org/2016/08/22/from-a-same-sex-attracted-muslim-between-denial-of-reality-and-distortion-of-religion/

CONVERSATION WITH RILEY

How Can Islam be Called a Religion of Peace?

Email #02 – From: Riley
Sent: Monday, April 11, 2011 3:25 a.m.
To: Ahmed Rashed

Dear Sir:
This is troubling and puzzling in light of your articles on the peacefulness of Islam. All sources are referenced.
http://frontpagemag.com/2011/04/08/destroying-one-koran-vs-destroying-many-christians-which-is-worse/
(Editor's note: This website is no longer working.)

Email #03 – From: Ahmed Rashed
Sent: Monday, April 11, 2011 11:52 a.m.
To: Riley

In the Name of God, the Most-Gracious, the Ever-Merciful:
The short answer is that this website is one of many whose sole purpose is to bash Muslims and confuse the public. Below is a 2005 quote from an article written by Louay Safi about these sites and the people behind them:

"Hardliners are engaged in cynical efforts to undermine the work of mainstream organizations who have been working for decades to develop Muslim institutions to nurture the needs of the growing American Muslim community, help the community integrate into the larger American society, and protect the civil rights and liberties of Muslims. Hardliners are busy in inventing Muslim organizations whose main missions are to roll back American Muslim achievements.

Daniel Pipes, whose whole career is built on bashing Muslims and confusing the public through half-truths and innuendos, is yet to find moderate Muslim organizations or leaders. He has accused every Muslim organization and leader of repute of extremism, militancy, and radicalism. His list of militant organizations includes: The Islamic Society of North America (ISNA), Muslim Public Affairs Council (MPAC), Council of American-Islamic Relations (CAIR), Islamic Circle of North America (ICNA), Muslim American Society (MAS), and others. Muslim organizations have for years been the subject of his attacks and accusations. He, most recently, added the newly founded

Progressive Muslim Union of North America (PMUNA) and the Center for the Study of Islam and Democracy (CSID) to the list.

Pipes collaborates with a group of off-centrists that includes David Horowitz, Kenneth Timmerman, Steve Emerson, and Steven Schwartz in attacking Islam and Muslims. The group employs smear tactics of "quotes taken out of context, guilt by association, errors of fact, and innuendo," and utilizes neo-conservative publications such as the Daily and Weekly Standards, National Review, Insight, and Front Page Magazine, to coordinate their attacks."

The full article is here:

http://www.theamericanmuslim.org/tam.php/features/arti cles/stephen_schwartz_center_on_islamic_pluralism/0018441

The website you quoted does link to actual events. We do not deny that. However, the website does not link to the mainstream Muslim *responses* to these events. There were so many formal statements made **against** terrorism, **against** violating the rights of non-Muslims, and **against** the acts described in your link. You can see them here:

http://theamericanmuslim.org/tam.php/features/articles/m uslim_voices_against_extremism_and_terrorism_part_i_fatwas/00 12209

Anyone who studies the actual teachings of Islam, especially its emphasis on personal accountability, usually comes to the conclusion that the acts of these Muslims are against the teachings of the Qur'an and the sayings of the Prophet.

Non-Muslims who live in a Muslim state are considered among those who have been promised safety, so any violation of their rights is a violation against the Prophet himself. There are Muslim scholars who went on Arab satellite and local TV to say this, to admonish Muslims to adhere to the teachings of the Prophet, and to command Muslims to respect the rights of non-Muslims living among them. They denounced the violence against the non-Muslims and their places of worship. However, this website and those like them do not include these responses.

Let me know if you would like more in-depth information or if you have any follow-up questions. I look forward to your response, Riley, and I hope to continue the discussion.

REMEMBER: With dialogue comes understanding.

May peace be with you,

Ahmed Rashed

**Email #04 – From: Riley
Sent: Tuesday, April 12, 2011 5:05 a.m.
To: Ahmed Rashed**

Ahmed,

Thank you for your response. I have great respect for people like you who volunteer for peaceful purposes for their faith or for charity. Let me start by saying that I am extremely reluctant to get into conversations that have anything to do with religion, because religion is faith, and many people of faith have strong beliefs that are unshakable. They can be offended by opinions that challenge their faith. Having said that, the sheer number of terrorist actions (actual or attempted) in the name of God by Muslims leads one to conclude that there is something terribly wrong. There are so many people quoting their holy book in the name of violence. Could this be because there are conflicting passages in the Koran, or subject to interpretation?

I read all of what you sent to me. I read a lot; I'm retired. Name-calling aside, I rarely read about Muslim countries and their leaders loudly condemning the many acts of terror. Now I know that there are a lot of Muslims in the world, so these terrorist actions are done by a small splinter group — although Muslim mobs (Afghanistan) go crazy and kill each other when one asshole here burns a Koran. People here burn American flags and put crosses in urine and call it "art." It's part of free speech, even though it can be repulsive to others. Think about those Christian Church members who go to funerals of American servicemen killed in action and yell that they deserved it. Disgusting, but allowed as free speech. Anyway, Americans are a reasonably tolerant people, as you know. Blacks, Jews, Muslims, etc., live here in peace with each other.

But the 9/11 atrocity was committed by Muslims; the shoe-bomber who was caught, thank God, before he could blow up an airplane was a Muslim; last year, a major in the US Army (a psychiatrist!) shot and killed several of his fellow soldiers while they were at dinner, while he shouted: "God is Great!" Finally, just last week, a Muslim man was caught in an FBI sting operation — he thought he was helping to attack several sites that would cause maximum number of deaths — in the name of Allah! The list goes on: England, subway bombings, attack on civilians in India by Muslim group from Pakistan.

What's going on with this? I don't think Americans in general are angry at all Muslims. Not yet. They are afraid. There is clearly a disconnect between your views and Muslim terrorists' views — you both cite your religion.

In peace,
Riley

Email #05 – From: Ahmed Rashed
Sent: Thursday, April 14, 2011 11:26 p.m.
To: Riley

In the Name of God, the Most-Gracious, the Ever-Merciful:
Hi Riley,

You bring up many good points, and I appreciate your being candid. There is so much negative information out there that it is easy to lose hope that dialogue can clear away the barriers to understanding. Let me address one specific incident before discussing the general issue of Muslims and violence. Regarding the reaction of the Afghans to the Qur'an-burning, check out this news excerpt:

"Indeed, the tragic murder of UN staff terrified the international community and there were confused reactions about the overall involvement in Afghanistan. But now, it is clear that Taliban insurgents had infiltrated the protest demonstration. Tolo News reported it was a

group of "reintegrated" Taliban who provoked people towards UNAMA office. Local Afghan staff of the UN said those killers had a very different dialect from Mazar. Later officials confirmed the 17 people arrested are from Kapisa and Kandahar and they have confessed being behind the pre-planned murders of UN staff. The UNAMA Chief Staffen De Mistura said there is evidence they were Taliban agitators with armed pistols who hunt down the UN workers. The BBC Farsi and Afghan media outlets also reported Taliban have claimed responsibility, though in their statement the militants did not express any regret on the murder of innocent people and called masses for further uprising.

The Cleric Council of Afghanistan, MPs and many others interviewed by TVs about the killings and riots have condemned it, except the Taliban. It is clear that Taliban do not recognize the UN as a neutral organization since the ISAF is UN-mandated force.

Every other day there is a protest demonstration against some issue in different cities, but rarely it turns violent. In Kandahar, where about 20 people died in last two days, the rioters burnt a girls' school, and those "protesting" had a white flag of the Taliban. While the demonstrations in Herat, Jalalabad and other cities went peaceful."

The full article is here:
http://outlookafghanistan.net/2011/04/murders-in-mazar-and-quran-burning/
(Editor's note: This website is no longer working.)

As my professor used to say, "by looking at contrasting cases, we can understand the specific case more deeply." So by looking at why all the **other** demonstrations in Afghanistan and around the world were peaceful but the one in Mazar was not, we understand that the actions were not representative of the Muslim masses, but rather a premeditated attack by opportunistic extremists.

Now for the general issue of why so many acts of violence and murder are done by Muslims and in the name of Islam in this day and age. I specifically say "this day and age" because these types of acts are something peculiar to the late 20th–early 21st century. The 19th, 18th, and 17th centuries saw none of these kinds of acts perpetrated by Muslims in the name of Islam. Even the 15th and 16th centuries saw Muslims doing no more than the usual Game of Empires that Asia and Europe were playing. So what is it that makes this day and age so different?

There are three threads that weave together to form the story we see today.

First, we have the genuine grievances of Muslim masses regarding what is going on in the Middle East. Specifically, this is referring to corrupt despotic dictators being propped up by Western powers and the state of Israel evicting hundreds of thousands of indigenous Muslim and Christian Arabs while oppressing millions more.

Second, we have the ignorance of most Muslims about the political aspects of their own faith. Terrorizing the civilian population, whether by individuals or states, can *never* be termed as jihad and can *never* be reconciled with the authentic teachings of Islam. The ends *NEVER* justify the means in Islam.

The Quran says: **God does not forbid you, regarding those who have not fought you in religion's cause, nor expelled you from your homes, that you should be kindly to them, and act justly towards them; surely God loves the just. God only forbids you as to those who have fought you in religion's cause, and expelled you from your homes, and have supported in your expulsion, that you should take them for allies. And whosoever takes them for allies, those are the evildoers. (60:8-9)**

So God REQUIRES that Muslims treat peaceful non-Muslims with goodness and equality.

Moreover, the declaration of war can only be given by someone who is responsible for the results of such a decision. It is the state authority that can declare war and make peace, not a group of shadowy guerillas with no home address. The Prophet led military expeditions in his capacity as leader of the city-state of Medina, and he always reminded them that it was only lawful to shed the blood of the armed soldiers who are actively fighting and trying to kill you. If they are not soldiers, or they are soldiers who have been disarmed, or they are soldiers who have surrendered, THEN IT IS FORBIDDEN TO KILL THEM.

The texts are very clear. I understand the frustration with US meddling and aggression in the Middle East. Most Muslims see the US foreign policy as a major obstacle to peace in the region. However, this frustration **does not justify** wanton attacks against civilians. Islamic law forbids this. And you cannot call yourself a good Muslim if you are willing to break Islamic law. That simply does not make sense.

Third and finally, we have the fact that the media amplifies the violent and sensational sheikhs that call for bloodshed and war while *ignoring* the sheikhs that call for restraint and justice and understanding. All this together means your typical Muslim youth, instead of going to his local preacher and asking what he can do about the sad state of the world, goes to the internet and finds the most virally circulated war-mongering sheikh. From this, he decides that the right thing to do is to start killing people. Those who actually ATTEND the mosques and listen to our scholars' lectures and ask questions and get answers do not come away with this understanding. It is those who listen to telecasts and web propaganda who become convinced that jihad means killing non-Muslims wherever they are by whatever means necessary.

I pray this sheds some light on some of the factors that cause the state of affairs we see in the world today. It is genuine grievances + widespread ignorance + amplified misinformation.

May peace be with you,
Ahmed

Email #06 – From: Riley
Sent: Sunday, April 17, 2011 5:11 p.m.
To: Ahmed Rashed

Hello Ahmed,
Could you recommend to me a good publication of the Koran in the English language (with annotations) for a lay person?

I am not interested in becoming a Muslim. I am interested in learning for myself what is motivating so many Muslims to take violent actions these days. I understand the Koran is for a Muslim like the Old Testament is for a Jew, or the New Testament is for a Christian. There has been so much violence against other Muslims (al-Qaida, Sunni/Shia) and against Jewish civilians (Jewish grocery store and synagogues in France), and slitting the throat of a priest in his church in France, and against other "infidels" (beheadings) and in USA.

In every one of these atrocities, Muslims proclaim that they are carrying out their work in the name of Allah.

I am the kind of person who prefers to go to the source when I look for answers; hence my request to you. Thank you for taking the time to respond to my request. Perhaps when I become more knowledgeable, I can have a conversation with you.

Sincerely,

Riley

Email #07 – From: Ahmed Rashed
Sent: Monday, April 18, 2011 10:37 a.m.
To: Riley

In the Name of God, the Most-Gracious, the Ever-Merciful:

Hi Riley,

When it comes to Qur'an translations, my favorite is M.A.S. Haleem's The Qur'an (Oxford World's Classics). This is an easy-to-read translation. However, it does not have much commentary or footnotes. For that I would recommend Yahya Emerick's The Holy Qur'an in Today's English. This is a huge book, over 600 pages, with extensive footnotes and background essays to really immerse the reader in what the context of each passage was.

May peace be with you,

Ahmed

With Dialogue Comes Understanding

CONVERSATION WITH EOIN

Can Muslims and Christians Ever Live in Harmony?

Email #02 – From: Eoin
Sent: Wednesday, August 10, 2011 8:07 a.m.
To: Ahmed Rashed

I appreciate that you would like to present Islam in a favorable and perhaps fair way, but when I read of injustices caused by Muslims in Egypt towards non-Muslims, it diminishes your effort. Furthermore, I've met many Muslims who believe in conspiracy theories. In fact, my understanding is that in Muslim countries, balanced news isn't available. Can you prove me wrong?

Peace be with you,

Eoin

Email #03 – From: Ahmed Rashed
Sent: Wednesday, August 10, 2011 12:14 p.m.
To: Eoin

In the Name of God, the Most-Gracious, the Ever-Merciful:

Dear Eoin,

There are good Muslims and there are bad Muslims. The definition of good Muslim and bad Muslim is what is in the Qur'an and the Sayings of the Prophet. If a Muslim does an act that the Qur'an or the Prophet say is bad, then that act is bad and that Muslim is acting against the teachings of Islam. For example, if someone recruits Christians from the church so they can go bomb an abortion clinic, it is not right to say "your Christian faith enlists young men to carry out these acts." These acts are clearly against the teachings of Christianity.

Likewise, the acts that you mentioned are against the teachings of Islam. Every major mainstream Islamic scholar in Egypt and around the world has been condemning these kinds of acts. Also, it is a fact that during the Egyptian popular uprising, Muslims and Christians took to the streets together. The Muslims formed a defensive ring around the Christians so they could hold their Sunday service in safety, and the Christians formed a defensive ring around the Muslims so they could hold their

Friday prayers in safety. Even after the uprising, when there were acts of intolerance against churches, major clerics and imams immediately spoke out on Egyptian media and to their congregations in sermons denouncing these acts. The Muslim and Christian leadership met and reaffirmed their commitment to peaceful coexistence and cooperation for the betterment of all Egyptian citizens.

The problem is that the sheer volume of media propaganda and misinformation against Islam drowns out the mainstream Muslim voice. While it is true that some Muslims do evil deeds, it is also true that certain media outlets emphasize those evil acts without balancing what the religion actually preaches and what the majority actually practice.

As for the tendency for Muslims to promote and believe in conspiracy theories, this is a result of growing up in a society where the government routinely lies to its people. The same thing happened to Americans after Watergate, but the US government did attempt to be transparent and forthright in the decades after. The Muslim governments never even tried. The Middle East still has not had an era of free information and corroborated media. Right now, Al-Jazeera is the only media outlet that challenges the "official" stories of the various Arab governments, but even they have their biases. Until free societies take hold in the Middle East (which many Muslims hope this Arab Awakening will lead to), and until there are more media outlets to compete with Al-Jazeera, the Muslim masses will continue to be skeptical of all information that is broadcast to them.

One of God's gifts to humanity is the gift of speech. It is by dialogue that we can come to greater understanding. I look forward to your reply, Eoin, so we may continue the discussion and dialogue.

May peace be with you,
Ahmed

Email #04 – From: Eoin
Sent: Wednesday, August 10, 2011 12:52 p.m.
To: Ahmed Rashed

Ahmed,

Thank you for returning my email.

I agree with you that the media often has an agenda. I have experienced this personally. My wife is from Ireland, and I lived there (as well as in Germany and Belgium). The British hold the Irish in contempt. As you may be aware, Northern Ireland has a long history of violence, and Roman Catholics, such as myself, were targeted by the British police and Military. Uneducated British citizens (or subjects) have long considered the Irish and Catholics in general to be beneath them. The British media is seldom honest with regards to the troubles in Northern Ireland, so I have empathy for the position of Muslims.

Here in the Southeastern US, protestant Christians are also hostile to Catholics because we are traditional Christians and we interpret the bible differently. I assume this is similar to the Sunni and Shia branches of Islam. So I do feel a sense of understanding of what Muslims must be experiencing.

Regarding the media, I don't expect them to treat anyone with fairness. I expect the media to push their agenda. I don't want you to think that I would treat Muslims with the same disdain that my people, Irish Catholics, have been treated. I would not. In fact, I feel a sense of kinship with Muslims. You are now experiencing what Catholics have endured for hundreds of years by our oppressors.

I would hope that Muslims would continue to make efforts to help bring justice to their countries. I am friends with Egyptian Christians in my town. They have been a source of information regarding the happenings in Egypt. They confirm some of what you have stated, but also have told me that Christians are persecuted in Egypt. They tell me that recently the wife of an Orthodox priest was kidnapped and that she "converted' to Islam while in custody. The Egyptian army won her release, only to have Muslims attack the church because they had "kidnapped' a Muslim — who was never Muslim in the first place.

Yes, I understand that I shouldn't blame everyone for the crimes of a few. The recent sexual scandals in my own church teach me that. There does, however, seem to be a prevailing hostility in Muslim countries towards non-Muslims. So, my question is: are there Muslim organizations willing to set the course straight so that everyone has equal rights and protection under the law in Muslim countries?

I think the best strategy is exactly that. Create justice and the injustice will be diminished. The responsibility for creating justice for all, including Muslims, in the US is my responsibility as it is all of our responsibility. I will, as i have always, do just that. Hopefully a sense of fairness and decency will prevail around the world.

I wish you the very best.

Peace be with you,

Eoin

Email #05 – From: Ahmed Rashed
Sent: Thursday, August 11, 2011 10:32 a.m.
To: Eoin

In the Name of God, the Most-Gracious, the Ever-Merciful:

Eoin,

You are quite welcome. It is through dialogue that understanding can flourish. I too hope that Muslims will continue to cultivate justice and equality in their countries. This is why many Muslims left their Muslim-majority homelands and migrated to the West. Ibn Taymiyah, a famous 13th century scholar, wrote the following in his book on divine justice and political ethics: *"God will support the Just nation, even if it is not Muslim; and He will not support the Unjust Nation, even if it is Muslim."*

This reality of injustice and corruption in the Middle East has caused many Muslims to see the need to reform their society so that God's blessings will return. This is true, from the most observant conservative Muslim imam to the casually observant Muslim youth. For this reason, I have hope for the future, and the reasons for my faith are below:

First is a letter from the Prophet Muhammad to the St. Catherine Monastery. Any Muslim who thinks they are being "good Muslims" by persecuting Christians is put to shame by this clear proof of what the Prophet intended.
http://www.islamicity.com/articles/Articles.asp?ref=IC0912-4019

The second link is a letter from a Western Christian activist who was on the ground during the Egyptian uprising. His letter shows the people's side of the story, far from politics and polemics.
https://www.christiancentury.org/article/2011-03/muslims-and-copts-together

I believe that Muslim organizations all around the world are ready and willing to engage in a path to universal justice and human rights. Saudi Arabia hosted its first interfaith conference, inviting a well-known Christian scholar for the first time in its history. This is a good sign. I also believe that Egyptian Muslims, with their long history of working and living side-by-side with Coptic Christians, are also willing and ready to form a new society based on law and justice, rather than connections and bribes. We all pray to God that He grants us His Grace and Mercy and Guidance, now more than ever.

May peace be with you,
Ahmed

Email #06 – From: Eoin
Sent: Thursday, August 11, 2011 10:54 a.m.
To: Ahmed Rashed

Ahmed,

These articles offered me hope that justice can be achieved. It was inspiring. I hope that the radical elements of Muslim countries lose their influence and that we can all live peacefully. I am at times skeptical but am more than willing to be won over.

Peace be with you,

Eoin

Email #07 – From: Ahmed Rashed
Sent: Tuesday, December 21, 2010 7:35 a.m.
To: Eoin

In the Name of God, the Most-Gracious, the Ever-Merciful:

Eoin,

I am glad we were able to offer you hope. It is a dark time we live in, but we are trying to push back against the ignorance and fear and hatred with patience and authentic information and knowledge.

As Muslims, we are required to believe that everything happens according to God's Plan and Wisdom. There is not a leaf that falls from a tree without His permission. We believe that any and all suffering is part of God's test for us on this Earth, as well as an admonishment for our sins and transgressions. It is this cycle of good times and bad times by which God tests the sincerity of His servants, to see if we will be thankful during the good times and steadfastly patient during the bad times.

If you have any further questions or concerns about Islam or Muslims, please feel free to contact me.

May peace be with you,

Ahmed

###

With Dialogue Comes Understanding

A Message From the Author

"You will never understand a man until you walk a mile in his shoes."

I thank you for walking a mile with me on my journey of interfaith conversations. It has always been my belief that understanding comes with dialogue, and I pray this book has added understanding and benefit to you. I would like to take this opportunity to share some reflections about these dialogues.

One of my earliest lessons as a WhyIslam volunteer was that there are three main types of visitors. The first type hates Islam and Muslims, no matter what we may say. They have a right to their opinion, and as the Qur'an says, "You are only responsible for conveying the message." So I learned to keep emotionally aloof, replying only with enough objective facts to address their issue or refute their accusations. This has the benefit of keeping the conversation from degenerating into unproductive arguments. While these visitors rarely turn over to reconciliation, it does happen occasionally, so it behooves us to keep a level head, to speak to the talking points, and to restrain from comments that will only lead to escalation.

The second type is supportive of Islam and Muslims and usually come requesting clarification and advice. For these visitors, I learned that they are hungry for details; therefore, it is okay to go more in depth, with tangential comments or background stories. These extra details add substance to the conversation and often lead to other lines of inquiry that these visitors find very valuable to them.

The third type is the truly undecided, and it is this type that provided the most memorable and soul-shifting conversations. To me, these visitors represent the essence of what we are trying to achieve: to touch the minds and hearts of those who do not know us and bring them from a position of not knowing about Islam and Muslims to a position of knowing Islam and Muslims. Even if they do not agree with us at the end of the conversation, what is important is that there was dialogue and the opportunity for improved understanding.

The last thing I learned is that sometimes people disengage and stop responding. You may have noticed a few times in this book that a conversation would end abruptly. While this is not satisfying, it is unfortunately the nature of email. Nobody is obligated to reply, and for this reason every reply is precious. Likewise, remember that "in real life," nobody is obligated to return your greeting or your salutation of peace; therefore, everyone who does respond to you — whether neighbor or classmate or coworker — is likewise precious.

If you enjoyed the book, please spread the word about it to your friends and contacts. If you have the time and inclination, it would be **great** if you would leave a review. Word-of-mouth is crucial for any author to succeed, so even if it is just a sentence or two, it would make all the difference and would be *very much* appreciated!

You can find more information and updates at our website WhatWouldAMuslimSay.net. Sign up to receive exclusive conversations that didn't make it into this book, free eBooks, my Islam101 slideshows, previews of upcoming books, and other relevant links and resources on Islam.

May peace be with you,
Ahmed Lotfy Rashed

The Qur'an Discussions

What Would A Muslim Say?

Volume 2

by

Ahmed Lotfy Rashed

Coming November 2017

If you loved WHAT WOULD A MUSLIM SAY *and can't wait for more, read on for a preview of the next book in the series.*

We met Winston in my first book "What Would a Muslim Say?" Winston asked many questions of a deep nature over the course of eleven months as he read through the Qur'an. This conversation was one of the most extensive exchanges I have ever had in my volunteer work. Due to the complex, intricate, and extended nature of the topics covered, this entire book will consist of my conversation with Winston.

Here is a taste of some of that extended conversation. . .

Email #42 – From: Winston
Sent: Sunday, May 15, 2011 7:37 p.m.

Hello Ahmed,

Thank you for responding to my previous questions. Could you please help me to understand the following ayahs from the Qur'an:

Regarding ayah 6:75, did Ibrahim (peace be upon him) became a Muslim after seeing the visible and invisible worlds? If Ibrahim (peace be upon him) gained Iman (faith) without witnessing miracles, then what were the circumstances or the event in which he (peace be upon him) became a believer?

Regarding ayah 6:116, does the verse apply only to a specific time period? If the ayah is addressed to every future generation, then that would mean Islam will never become the religion for a majority of people. If Islam were to become the largest religion in the world, then this verse would be a contradiction.

May peace be with you,
Winston

Email #43 – From: Ahmed Rashed
Sent: Tuesday, May 17, 2011 12:34 p.m.

In the Name of God, Most Gracious, Most Merciful:

Hello Winston,

Ibrahim (pbuh) was a natural monotheist, like all the other prophets. His heart and nature were in tune with the signs all around him that there IS a creator and that this creator must be ONE and TRANSCENDENT. The story related in this passage (verses 74-82) are about how he pondered one night and translated this intuition into a rational argument. This rational argument both solidified his faith and provided grounding to confront his polytheistic community.

Ayah 6:116 was revealed specifically to address the Prophet's arguments with pagans around him. It is also applicable to all later generations, as the Prophet prophesied, *"Islam began as something strange and it will end as something strange, so Glad Tidings to the strangers!"* The point is that the right thing for a truth-seeker is not to consider what way the majority of the people are following, because that is based on guesswork instead of knowledge. Their beliefs, theories, philosophies, principles of life and laws are the result of guesswork and are, therefore, sure to mislead. In contrast to that, the way of life with which God is pleased can only be the Way that God Himself has taught. Therefore, the seeker-after-truth should adopt that way and steadfastly follow it, even though he is left alone on it.

The Prophet also was instructed in the Qur'an that most people will NOT believe. You will read verses that imply this meaning in several chapters as you go thru the Qur'an. This is true at any instant in time, and it is definitely true for all mankind cumulatively. The Prophet compared righteous believers and wicked disbelievers like the head of a man who is beginning to gray; most hairs are black (evil), a few are white (good), and several are in various stages of gray (in between).

Note that the issue is not Muslim vs. non-Muslim *per se*, but rather it is about those who are on the right guidance and right behavior. Many, many Muslims in this age, as in previous ages, do bad things, so their label of Muslim does not make them automatically "rightly guided."

May peace be with you,
Ahmed

Email #46 – From: Winston
Sent: Tuesday, May 24, 2011 6:24 p.m.

Hello Ahmed,

Thank you for responding to my previous questions. Could you please help me to understand the following ayahs of the Qur'an.

Regarding ayah 7:11–25, God discusses how He created two human beings and placed them in paradise, and these people were allowed everything except the fruit from a tree. Iblis beguiled them into eating the fruit, and God punished the first humans by sending them to live on Earth. That is the origin of mankind, according to Islam, but over the past two hundred years people have developed a theory of our origin based on observation and testing. There is an enormous amount of biological and archeological evident that demonstrates that people evolve from simpler organisms that evolve from ever more simpler creatures in a lineage spanning about a billion years. Since there is an apparent contradiction between scientific knowledge and the revealed knowledge, then the following question needs to be asked. **Does God wish to make it impossible to prove with objective evidence that all the supernatural events in the Qur'an actually occurred?** The Prophet Muhammad (peace be upon him) seems to emphasize that faith should not require proof in the following authentic Hadith:

Narrated Abu Huraira: The Prophet (peace be upon him) said: *"There was no Prophet among the Prophets but was given miracles because of which people had belief, but what I have been given is the Divine Revelation which God has revealed to me. So I hope that my followers will be more than those of any other Prophet on the Day of Resurrection."* (Hadith No. 379, Vol. No. 9, Sahih Al-Bukhari)

If the last Prophet (peace be upon him) expected his followers to have faith that is not supported by evidence, such as performing miracles, then that appears to imply that God will not allow anything to exist that can objectively prove these extraordinary events in the Qur'an. I am not a Muslim, so it is possible that I am making false assumptions about this Hadith and ayahs 7:11–25. However, it seems to me that the consequence of having an objective way of verifying these miracles is that there will be no struggle to obey God. In other words, the inner jihad would not exist. If the physical proof was discovered, then individuals will convert to Islam in order to adapt to circumstances, just as an animal adapts to the weather in order to survive. This decision becomes necessary if there is evidence that guarantees success in this world and in an afterlife. Any decision that is optional, by definition, would become a struggle to perform, because there is no evidence that guarantees success. Therefore, evidence of faith contradicts a struggle to have faith.

May peace be with you,
Winston

.... *End of Excerpt* ....

TOP 15 TOUGH QUESTIONS ON ISLAM

AHMED LOTFY RASHED

Get your FREE copy when you sign up to the author's email list!

GET IT HERE:
www.WhatWouldAMuslimSay.net

About the Author

Ahmed Lotfy Rashed was born in Egypt and raised in Maryland. He studied physics at the University of Maryland Baltimore County. While there, he was on the Speakers Bureau for the Muslim Students' Association. He continued his education in Pennsylvania, earning his Masters' degree at Bryn Mawr College.

During his three years of graduate study, he served as Public Relations Officer for the Muslim Students' Association. It was at this time that Ahmed started talking about Islam at various churches, temples, and schools. He became known for his informal and approachable demeanor. His ability to break down complex religious and historical contexts for audiences earned him high reviews. He also taught math and science at the local Islamic School. In addition, he led the Youth Committee of the local mosque in Villanova. Soon after graduating, he married and found employment in Boston as a research engineer.

Since coming to Boston in 2004, he has been an active volunteer at several mosques in the Greater Boston Area. He has been the head instructor for the local Islam101 class since 2006. Also, he has been a volunteer for WhyIslam.org since 2009. He has presented Islam at schools and churches, and he has hosted visits to several major mosques in the area.

Ahmed continues to work and live in the Greater Boston Area with his wife and three children. In his spare time, he likes to read about comparative religions, Islamic law, Islamic history, and military history. He also has a weakness for fantasy and science fiction novels — a problem of which his wife is still trying very hard to cure him.

Online References

The Authenticity of the Qur'an
http://www.ilaam.net/Articles/AuthenticQuran.html

Biblical Prophecies on the Advent of Muhammad
http://www.islam-guide.com/frm-ch1-3.htm

The Qur'an is Amazing
http://www.islam101.com/science/GaryMiller.html

Stories of New Muslims
http://islamicweb.com/begin/newMuslims/

Topic index of the Qur'an
http://www.islamicity.com/mosque/TOPICI.HTM

The Holy Qur'an by Abdullah Yusuf Ali
http://www.islamicity.com/mosque/Surai.htm

What they say about Islam, the Qur'an and Muhammad
http://www.islamicity.com/Mosque/aboutislam.htm

Islamic Golden Age
http://en.wikipedia.org/wiki/Islamic_Golden_Age

Christian Modesty
http://www.chapellibrary.org/pdf-english/cmod.pdf

Muslims Condemn Terrorist Attacks
http://www.muhajabah.com/otherscondemn.php

Stephen Schwartz and the Center on Islamic Pluralism
http://www.theamericanmuslim.org/tam.php/features/arti
cles/stephen_schwartz_center_on_islamic_pluralism/0018441

Print References

An Introduction to the Sciences of the Qur'aan (Abu Ammaar Yasir Qadhi)

A Thematic Commentary on the Qur'an (Muhammed al-Ghazali)

Muhammad: His Life Based on the Earliest Sources: Revised Edition (Martin Lings)

MUHAMMAD: A Biography of the Prophet (Karen Armstrong)

War and Peace in the Life of the Prophet Muhammad (sws) (Zakaria Bashier)

The History of Islam: 3-Volume Hardcover Set (Akbar Shah Najeebabadi)

The Evolution of Fiqh (Dr. Abu Ameenah Bilal Philips)

The Concise Presentation of the Fiqh of the Sunnah and the Noble Book (Dr. Abdul-Azeem Badawi)

Ibn Taymeyah's Essay on the Jinn (Demons): 2nd Edition (Abu Ameenah Bilal Philips)

Even Angels Ask: A Journey to Islam in America (Jeffrey Lang)

On the Boundaries of Theological Tolerance in Islam (Dr. Sherman A. Jackson)

Studies in Hadith Methodology & Literature (M.M. Azami)

Islam from Within (Kenneth Cragg and Marston Speight)

Made in the USA
Middletown, DE
13 July 2020

12727321R00089